A REFERENCE FOR CHORD VOICINGS WITH PRACTICE ROUTINES

HAL LEONARD'S
JAZZ
GUITAR CHORD
THESAURUS

BY KIRK TATNALL

ISBN 978-1-4768-1335-6

HAL•LEONARD®
CORPORATION

7777 W. BLUEMOUND RD. P.O. BOX 13819 MILWAUKEE, WI 53213

In Australia Contact:
Hal Leonard Australia Pty. Ltd.
4 Lentara Court
Cheltenham, Victoria, 3192 Australia
Email: ausadmin@halleonard.com.au

Visit Hal Leonard Online at
www.halleonard.com

ABOUT THE AUTHOR

Photo by Gene Steinman

Since the age of three and a half years old, Kirk Tatnall has been chasing music via his favorite vehicle: the guitar. In addition to authoring instructional books for Hal Leonard, Kirk continues to perform, compose, record and release original music, teach guitar, and lend his playing to other artists and various commercial music sessions. For more details please visit **www.kirktatnall.com**.

Table of Contents

CHAPTER 3: Drop 3 Voicings, Linear Movement

CHAPTER 4: Drop 3 Voicings, Diagonal Movement

CHAPTER 5: ii–V–I Melodic Patterns

CHAPTER 6: Applying Your New Chords

INTRODUCTION

Welcome to the *Jazz Guitar Chord Thesaurus*. As most of us journey along the path of learning jazz guitar, we develop a vocabulary of chords that mostly have the root in the bass. The goal of this book is to provide a clear cut path to learning all the inversions of seventh chords by using the two main building blocks of jazz harmony: major and minor ii–V–I chord progressions.

HOW TO USE THIS BOOK

To become fluent in the language of jazz and music in general, it is proven that one must develop equality of all twelve keys. The goal of this book is not only to provide a reference for learning chord fingerings, but to offer a daily practice routine for increasing the vocabulary of chords with which the guitarist has to work.

The first task is to simply wrap your brain and fingers around the chords that are new to you. Work each new section of chords slowly, making sure you cleanly finger the notes. Absorbing the sounds and fingerings is of the utmost importance. Speed will come later, as we are in this for the long haul. Daily repetition in a short practice session (approximately twenty minutes) is key to absorbing the new chords and much more effective than spending hours one day and none the next.

Once you have learned the basic fingerings of each set of chords, the idea is to play one key from each section of the book every day, keeping track of what you played the previous day. In the very beginning, it may take an entire practice session to play one exercise, but as you develop your vocabulary through repetition, you will eventually be able to play one exercise from each section in the book in one sitting. Moving the voicings linearly, diagonally, and through melodic ii–V–I patterns, along with the daily rotation of keys, will quickly give you new options to use while improvising.

Twenty Minute Chord Practice Routine

1. Pick a key of the day.
2. Play an exercise in that key from each section of the book.
3. Play one page of melodic ii–V–I patterns from Chapter 5 (a different one each day.)
4. Apply your new vocabulary by playing the examples in Chapter 6 or any music you may be playing.

Please remember this process will take time and perseverance. Some of these fingerings might remind you of how hard it was the first time you tried an open C chord, but they will become that easy too. The final step in learning a new word is to actually speak with it, and the same holds true with these new chord voicings. Good luck!

CHAPTER ONE

DROP 2 VOICINGS, LINEAR MOVEMENT

As we embark upon learning these new chords, let's take a minute to learn where they come from. A *drop 2* voicing is created by lowering the second highest voice of a standard closed-voiced seventh chord by one octave. In addition to the sound it creates, this enables fingering otherwise impossible chords on the guitar.

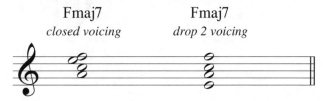

Voicing chords in this manner allows the playing of four-note seventh chords on three sets of adjacent strings.

STRING SET 4321

We're going to start with the top four strings, which is the string set 4321. Let's learn the first set of fingerings by playing each chord quality found in a ii–V–I: a major seventh, dominant seventh, and minor seventh. We'll play all these chords with F as the root for now, but afterward we'll play an exercise that makes use of the form in different ii–V–I progressions.

Major ii–V–I Chords: m7, 7, maj7

Play each set of these chords up and down the guitar while acclimating yourself to the fingerings. Note that the top note of each voicing is identified above the grid.

Minor Seven

Root
1 1 1 1

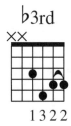
♭3rd
1 3 2 2

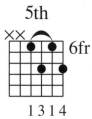
5th
1 3 1 4

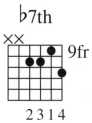
♭7th
2 3 1 4

Dominant Seven

Root
1 2 1 1

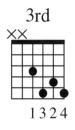
3rd
1 3 2 4

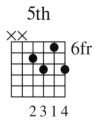
5th
2 3 1 4

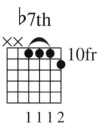
♭7th
1 1 1 2

Major Seven

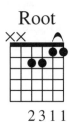
Root
2 3 1 1

3rd
1 3 3 3

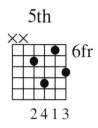
5th
2 4 1 3

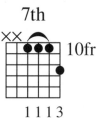
7th
1 1 1 3

When you feel ready to move forward, play the exercises on the next two pages, putting the proper chord under the melody note that is written. In addition to learning your voicings, you will be learning to harmonize a melody on sight. A frame showing the first chord of each measure is provided to ensure you get off on the right foot.

Major ii–V–I Exercise: String Set 4321

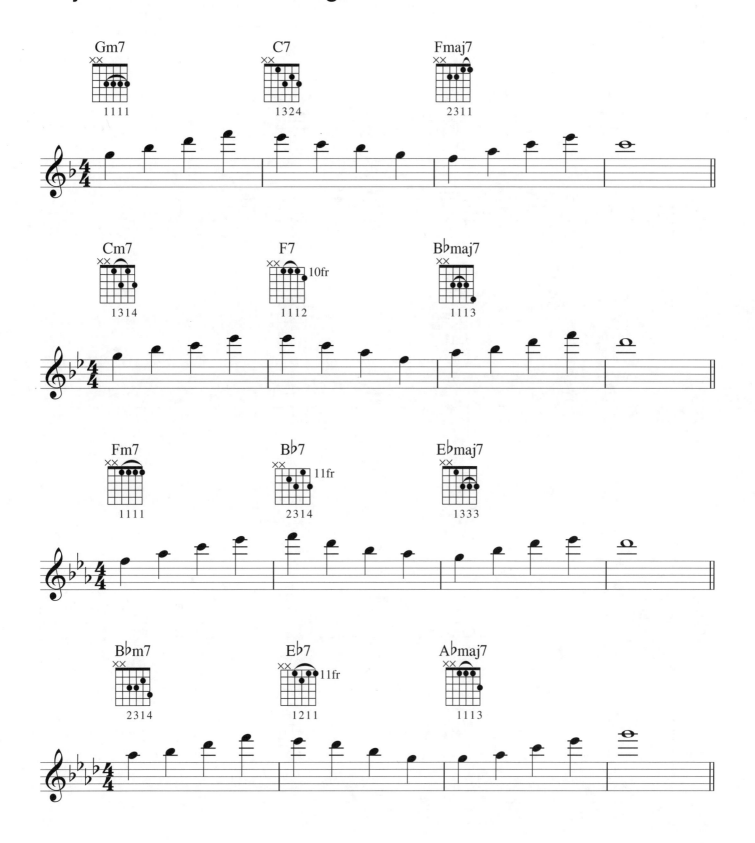

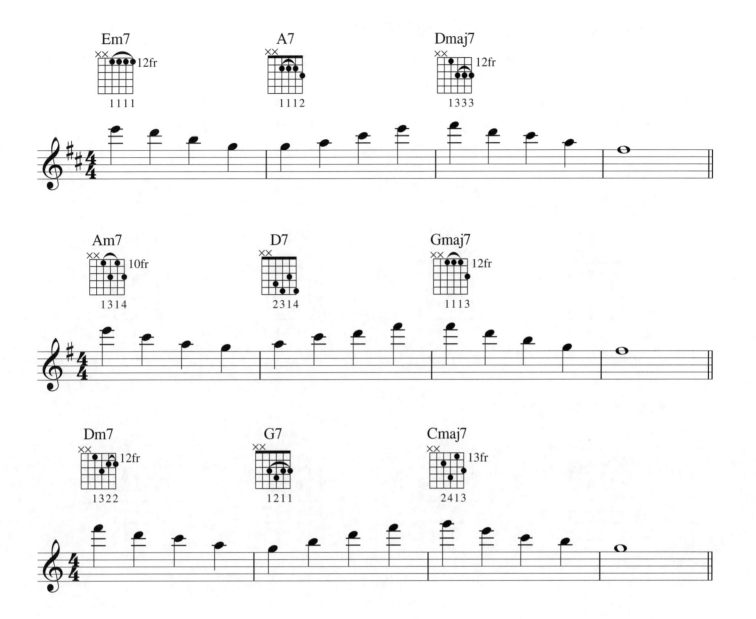

Minor ii–V–i Chords: m7♭5, V7♯5, m7

Now that we've learned the voicings for major ii–V I progressions, we'll explore what happens when we resolve to a minor chord. The 5th is lowered on the ii chord, creating a m7♭5 chord, but it's raised on the V chord, creating an augmented chord: a 7♯5. Again, play these voicings up and down the neck as F chords until you are reasonably comfortable with the fingerings and then proceed to the exercises.

Minor Seven Flat Five

Root

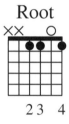

2 3 4

♭3rd

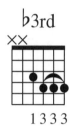

1 3 3 3

♭5th

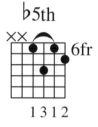

1 3 1 2

♭7th

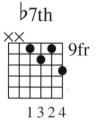

1 3 2 4

Augmented Seven

Root

1 3 4 2

3rd

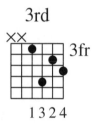

1 3 2 4

♯5th

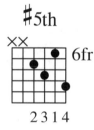

2 3 1 4

♭7th

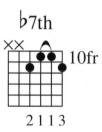

2 1 1 3

Minor Seven

Root

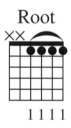

1 1 1 1

♭3rd

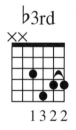

1 3 2 2

5th

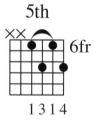

1 3 1 4

♭7th

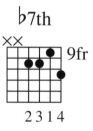

2 3 1 4

Minor ii–V–i Exercise: String Set 4321

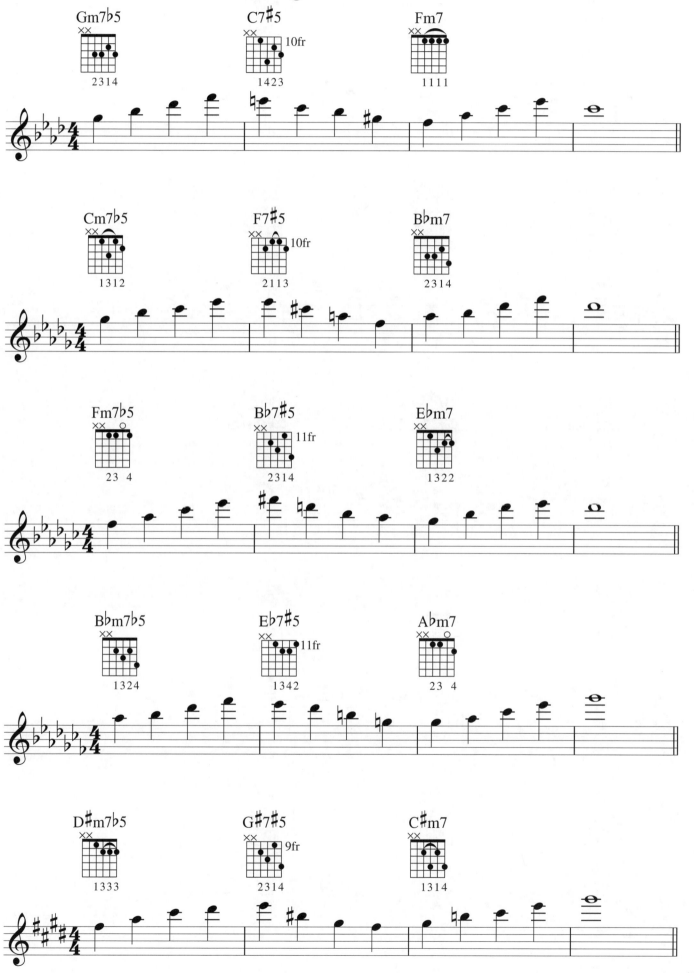

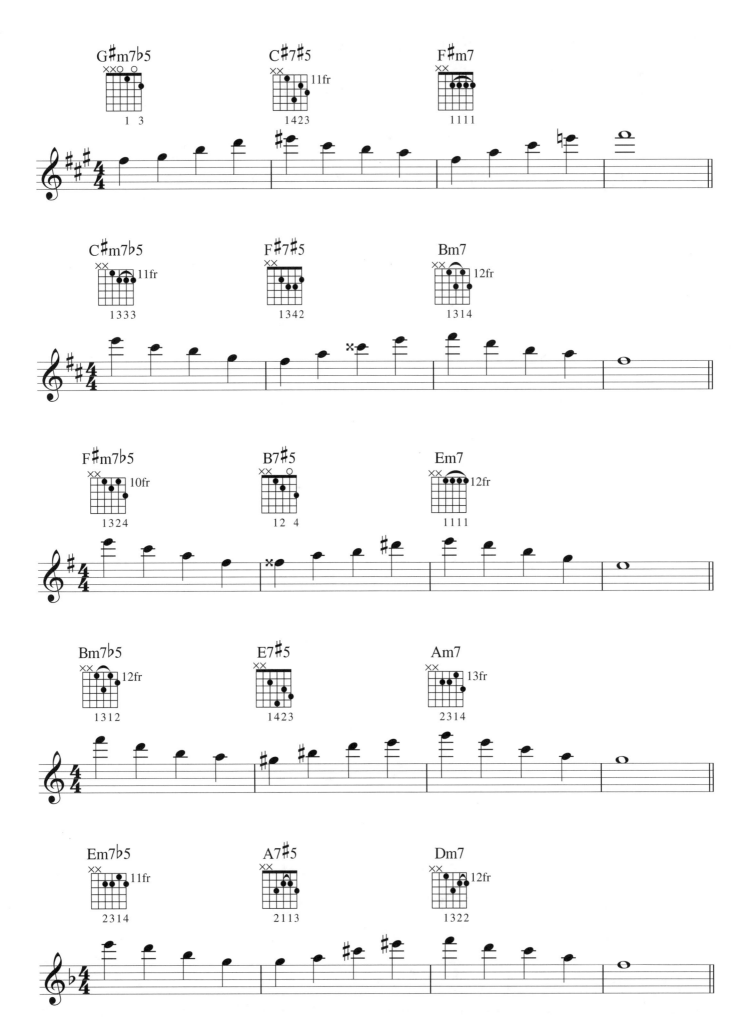

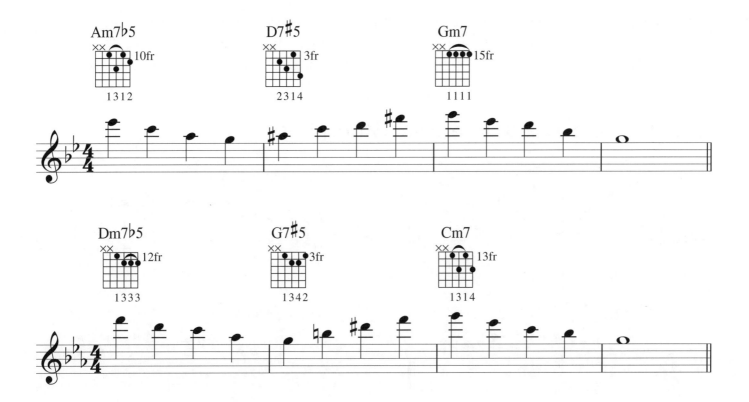

Diminished Seventh Chords

The diminished seventh chord serves several musical functions. Since it is constructed by stacking minor 3rd intervals, the chord is completely symmetrical. Any note of the chord can be the root, and there is only one fingering to learn per set of strings. Observe the example showing how the drop 2 voicing is created and try the fingering.

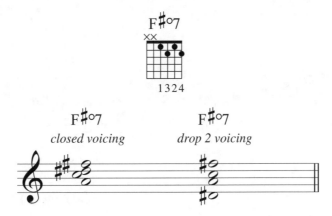

A very important function of the diminished chord in jazz, beyond being a passing chord, is as a 7♭9 sound on the V chord. This is accomplished by playing a diminished seventh a half step above the root of the V. Looking at the example shown below, observe how, when analyzed top to bottom as an F chord, we end up with all the key ingredients of F7, except we have the ♭9th (G♭) instead of the root (F).

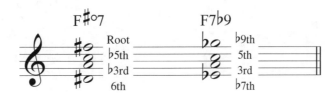

This is an incredibly useful chord substitution, and the exercises below are spelled to reflect the harmony of the 7♭9 chord. It may help you find these chords quickly in a real world situation if you use the ♭9th, 3rd, 5th, and ♭7th to visually line them up on your guitar. Play one of these exercises every day, depending on which of the twelve keys you are on at the moment.

Diminished Seventh Exercise: String Set 4321

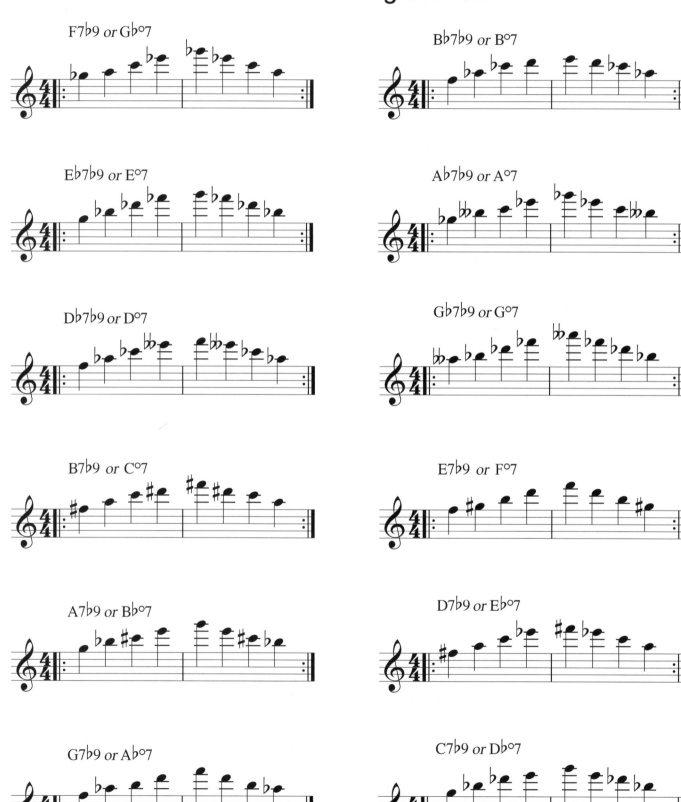

STRING SET 5432

While these chords are constructed identically on paper to the chord set we just learned, the asymmetrical tuning of the guitar requires us to learn new fingerings to play these on the middle string set. In the case of our major seventh chord, there are instances where stretching your pinky finger out to the seventh may not be possible. At any time, you can substitute a major sixth chord instead. Learn these fingerings up and down the neck in D and then work through the following exercises and add them to your one-key-per-day practice routine.

Major ii–V–I Chords: m7, 7, maj7

Minor Seven

Root	♭3rd	5th	♭7th
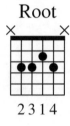	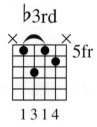	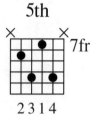	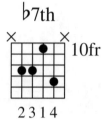
2 3 1 4	1 3 1 4	2 3 1 4	2 3 1 4

Dominant Seven

Root	3rd	5th	♭7th
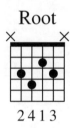	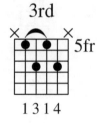	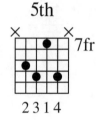	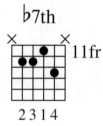
2 4 1 3	1 3 1 4	2 3 1 4	2 3 1 4

Major Seven

Root	3rd	5th	7th
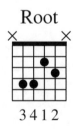	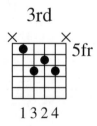	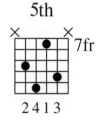	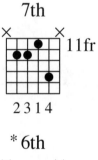
3 4 1 2	1 3 2 4	2 4 1 3	2 3 1 4

*6th

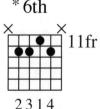

2 3 1 4

*Optional substitute
for major 7th.*

Major ii–V–I Exercise: String Set 5432

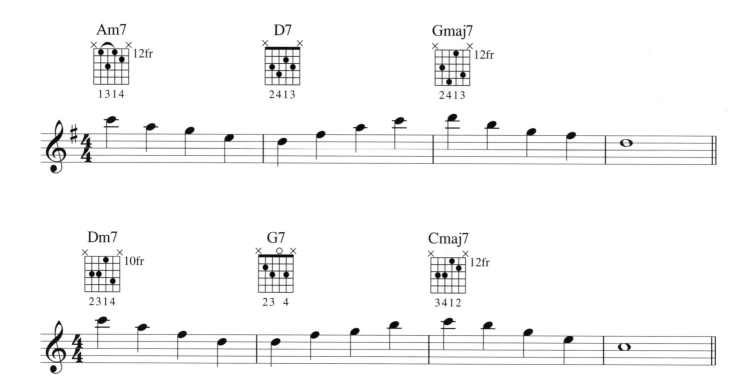

Minor ii–V–i Chords: m7♭5, V7♯5, m7

Just like our first set of chords, to play minor ii–V I progressions we need to raise the 5th of the V chord and lower the 5th of the ii chord. Take your time absorbing the new fingerings and add the following exercises to your daily practice. Again, all these chords are first presented here with D as the root.

Minor Seven Flat Five

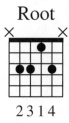
Root

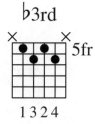
♭3rd

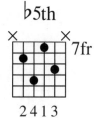
♭5th

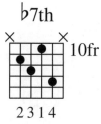
♭7th

Augmented Seven

Root

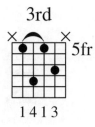
3rd

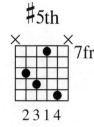
♯5th

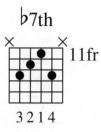
♭7th

Minor Seven

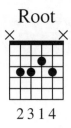
Root

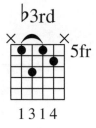
♭3rd

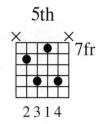
5th

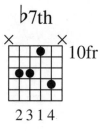
♭7th

Minor ii–V–i Exercise: String Set 5432

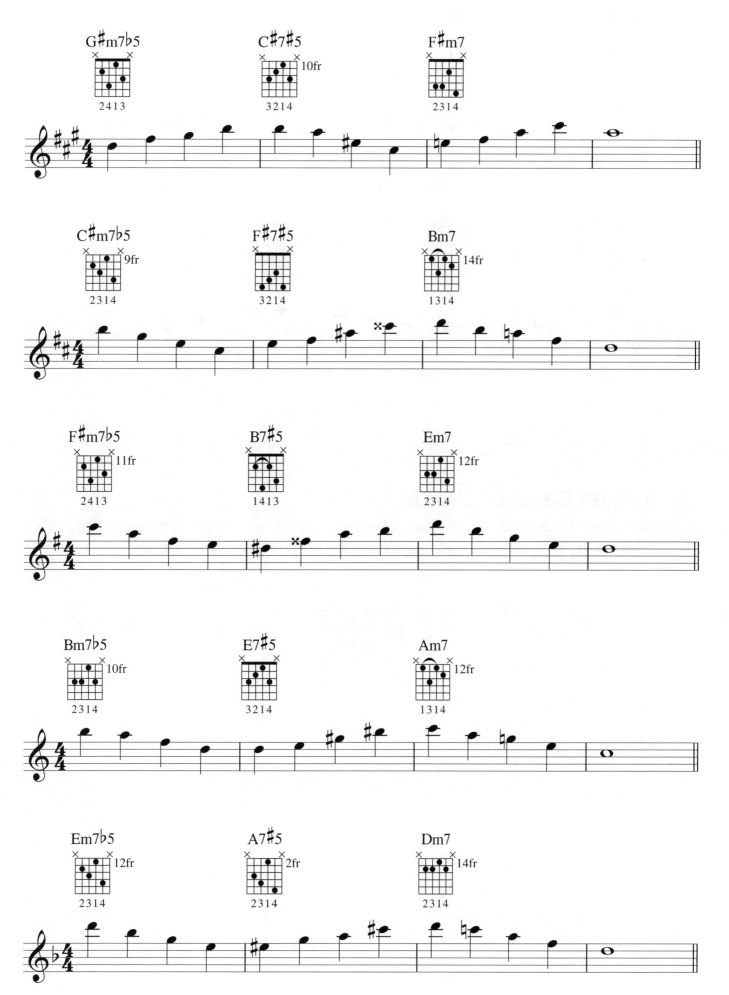

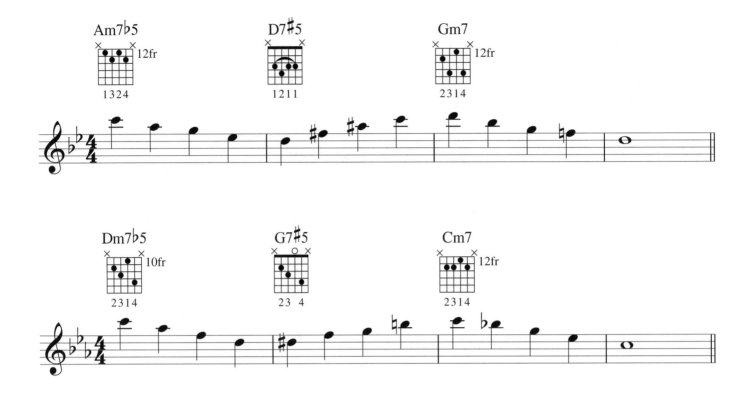

Diminished Seventh Chords

When moving the diminished chord to our next set of strings, the same concepts apply from our first group. The symmetrical nature of the chord again provides us with only one new fingering to learn.

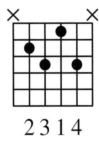

The following exercises are spelled to reflect the harmony of a 7♭9 chord, reinforcing the concept of playing a diminished chord a half step above the root to create that sound. Try thinking of the arpeggio's scale degrees (♭9th, 3rd, 5th, ♭7th) as you play the following exercises.

Diminished Seventh Exercise: String Set 5432

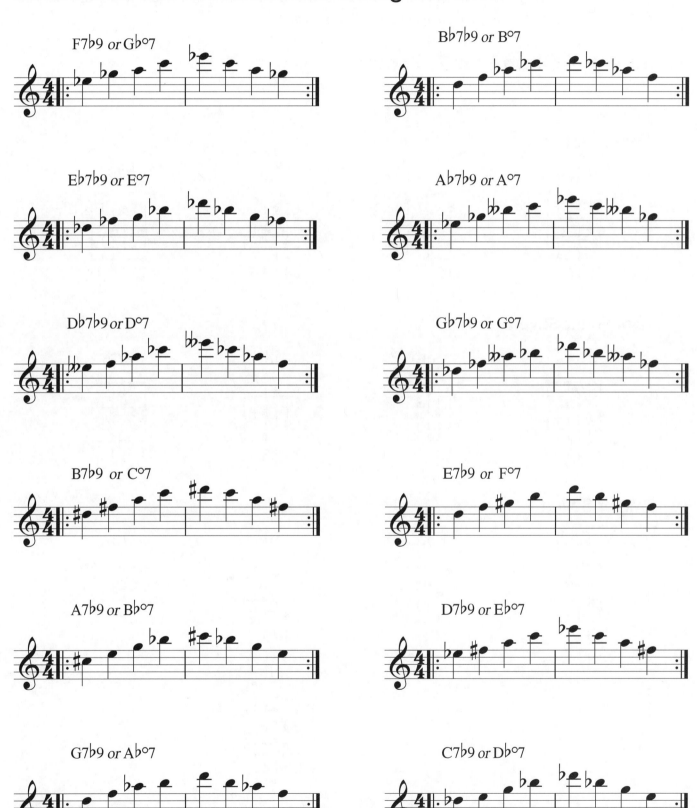

STRING SET 6543

Moving down to our lowest group of strings introduces us to our final set of drop 2 chord voicings. In this set of chords, the major seventh voicing with the 5th in the melody can be an awkward stretch. Substituting a major sixth chord can be a good alternative and can be applied using your own judgment. Follow the concepts you used learning the first two sets of chords and add these into your one-key-per-day practice routine. All of these chords will first be presented here with A as the root.

Major ii–V–I Chords: m7, 7, maj7

Minor Seven

Root	♭3rd	5th	♭7th
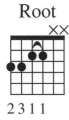	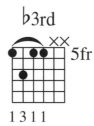	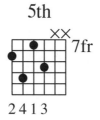	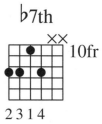
2 3 1 1	1 3 1 1	2 4 1 3	2 3 1 4

Dominant Seven

Root	3rd	5th	♭7th
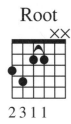	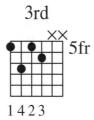	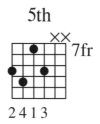	
2 3 1 1	1 4 2 3	2 4 1 3	2 3 1 4

Major Seven

Root	3rd	5th	7th
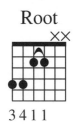	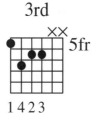	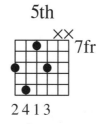	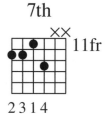
3 4 1 1	1 4 2 3	2 4 1 3	2 3 1 4

* 5th

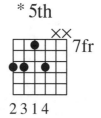

2 3 1 4

*Alternative major sixth voicing for major 7th with 5th on top.

Major ii–V–I Exercise: String Set 6543

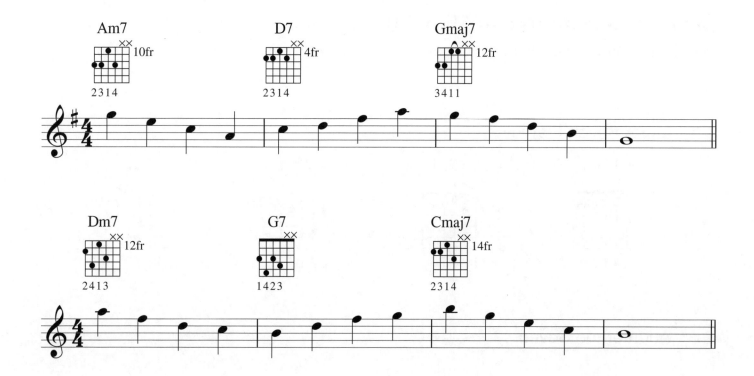

Minor ii–V–i Chords: m7♭5, V7♯5, m7

Here are the chords of the minor ii–V–i progression, again all presented first here with A as the root.

Minor Seven Flat Five

Root
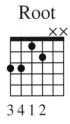
3 4 1 2

♭3rd
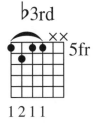
5fr
1 2 1 1

♭5th
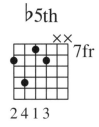
7fr
2 4 1 3

♭7th
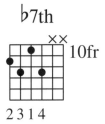
10fr
2 3 1 4

Augmented Seven

Root

2 4 3 1

3rd
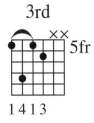
5fr
1 4 1 3

♯5th
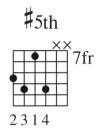
7fr
2 3 1 4

♭7th
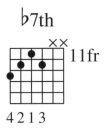
11fr
4 2 1 3

Minor Seven

Root
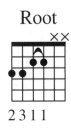
2 3 1 1

♭3rd
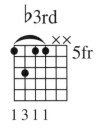
5fr
1 3 1 1

5th
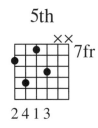
7fr
2 4 1 3

♭7th
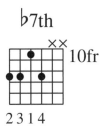
10fr
2 3 1 4

Minor ii–V–i Exercise: String Set 6543

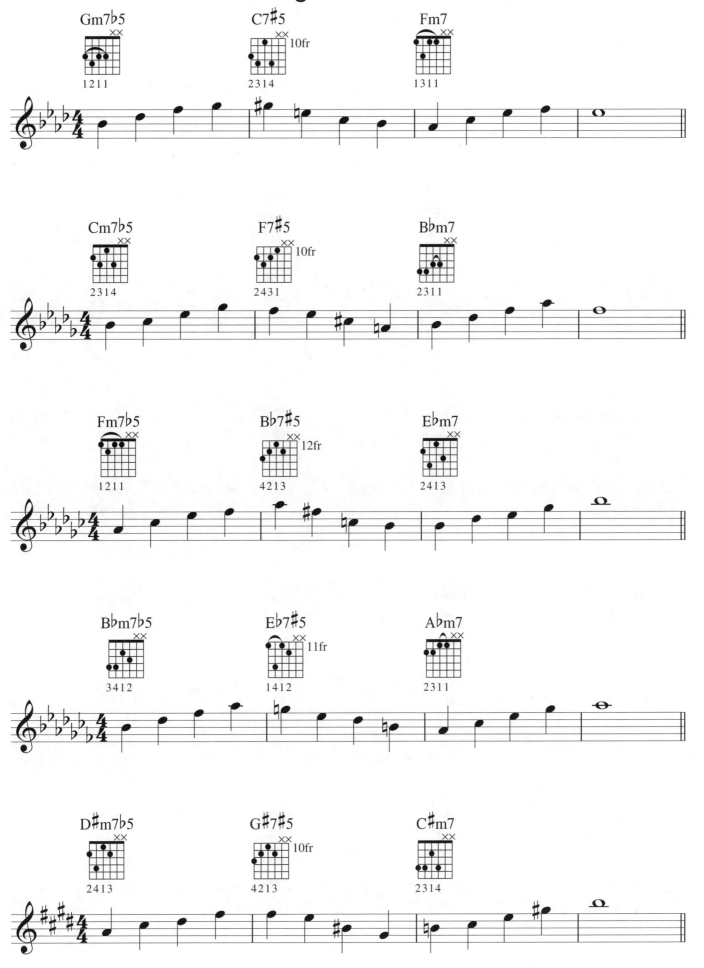

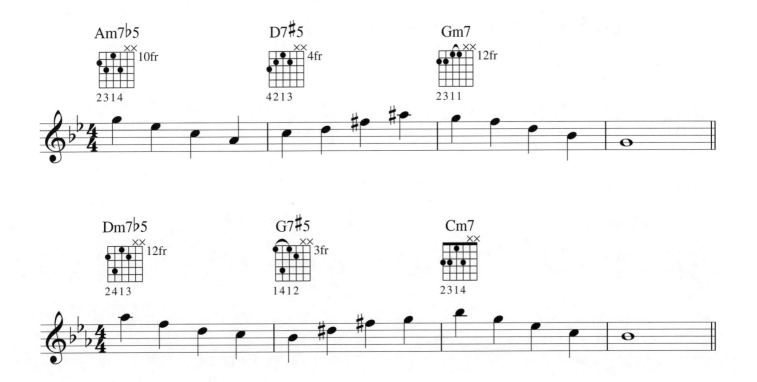

Diminished Seventh Chords

Again, the symmetrical nature of the diminished chord provides us with only one new fingering to learn on this final adjacent string set.

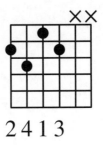

Diminished Seventh Exercise: String Set 6543

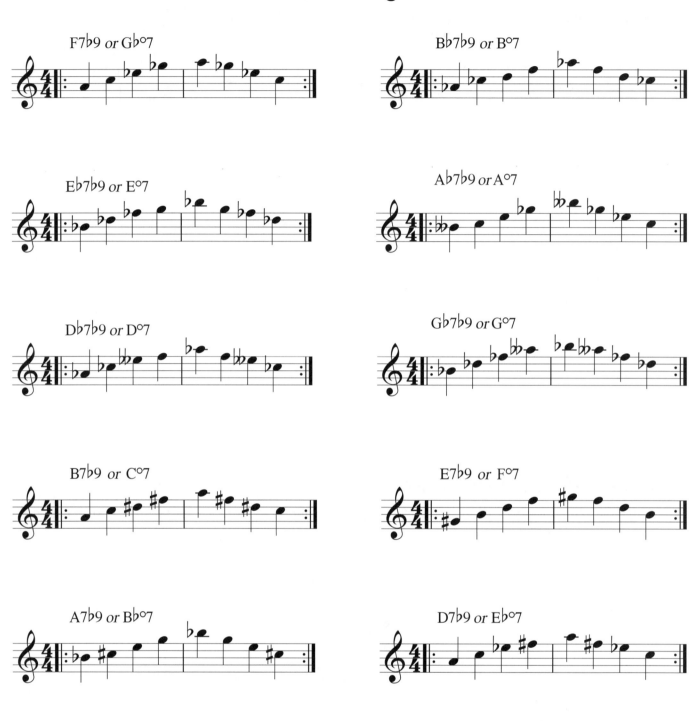

CHAPTER TWO

DROP 2 VOICINGS, DIAGONAL MOVEMENT

While moving in a linear fashion along the neck of the guitar is essential, it is equally important to be able to stay in one area of the neck and switch between chords on different sets of strings. We will refer to this as *diagonal movement*, since the chords move in diagonal lines towards the nut as you play the inversions. We will observe how this works over the next several pages by starting each chord quality from each of its chord tones in F. When you are ready, add one key per day from the ii–V I exercises in this chapter to your daily practice routine.

Diagonal Pattern Root–7th–5th

Fmaj7

Root   7th   5th

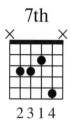
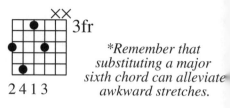

2 3 1 1   2 3 1 4   2 4 1 3

Remember that substituting a major sixth chord can alleviate awkward stretches.

F7

Root   ♭7th   5th

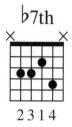
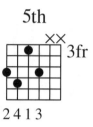

1 2 1 1   2 3 1 4   2 4 1 3

Fm7

Root   ♭7th   5th

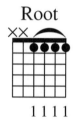
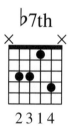
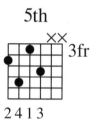

1 1 1 1   2 3 1 4   2 4 1 3

F7♯5

Root   ♭7th   ♯5th

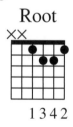
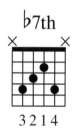
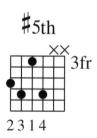

1 3 4 2   3 2 1 4   2 3 1 4

Fm7♭5

Root   ♭7th   ♭5th

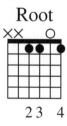
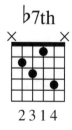
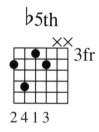

2 3   4   2 3 1 4   2 4 1 3

F7♭9/F♯°7

♭9th   ♭7th   5th

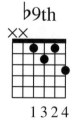
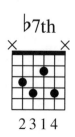
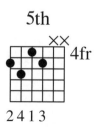

1 3 2 4   2 3 1 4   2 4 1 3

Diagonal Pattern 3rd–Root–7th

Fmaj7

3rd	Root	7th
	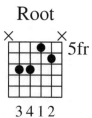	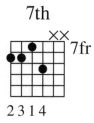
1 3 3 3	3 4 1 2	2 3 1 4

F7

3rd	Root	♭7th
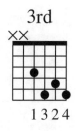	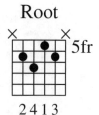	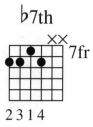
1 3 2 4	2 4 1 3	2 3 1 4

Fm7

♭3rd	Root	♭7th
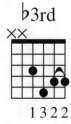	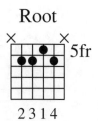	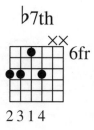
1 3 2 2	2 3 1 4	2 3 1 4

F7♯5

3rd	Root	♭7th
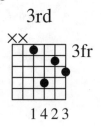	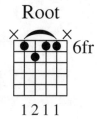	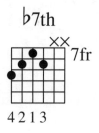
1 4 2 3	1 2 1 1	4 2 1 3

Fm7♭5

♭3rd	Root	♭7th
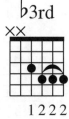	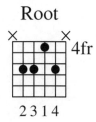	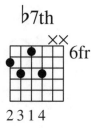
1 2 2 2	2 3 1 4	2 3 1 4

F7♭9/F♯°7

3rd	♭9th	♭7th
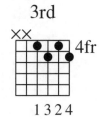	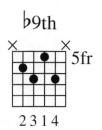	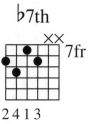
1 3 2 4	2 3 1 4	2 4 1 3

Diagonal Pattern 5th–3rd–Root

Fmaj7

5th   3rd   Root

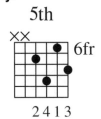 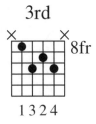 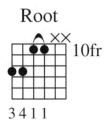

F7

5th   3rd   Root

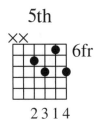 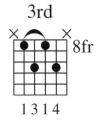 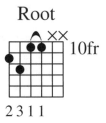

Fm7

5th   ♭3rd   Root

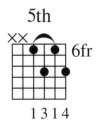 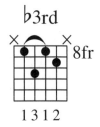 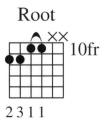

F7♯5

♯5th   3rd   Root

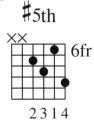 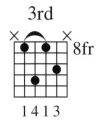 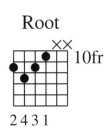

Fm7♭5

♭5th   ♭3rd   Root

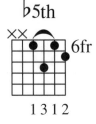 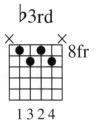 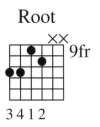

F7♭9/F♯°7

5th   3rd   ♭9th

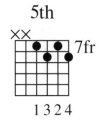 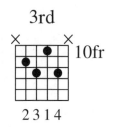 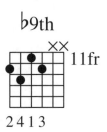

Diagonal Pattern 7th–5th–3rd

Fmaj7

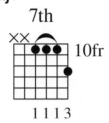

F7

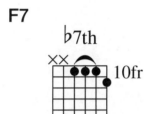

Fm7

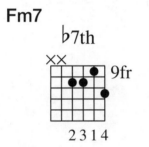

F7♯5

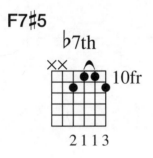

Fm7♭5

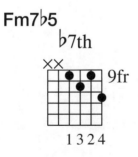

F7♭9/F♯°7

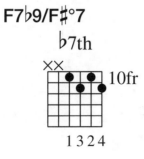

ii–V–I Drop 2 Diagonals Exercise in F

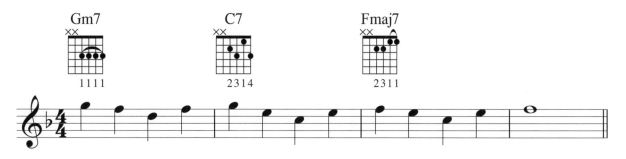

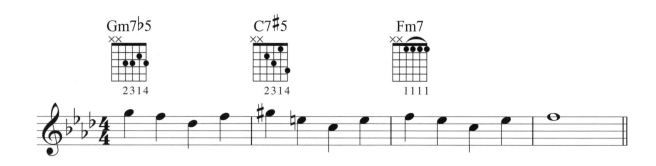

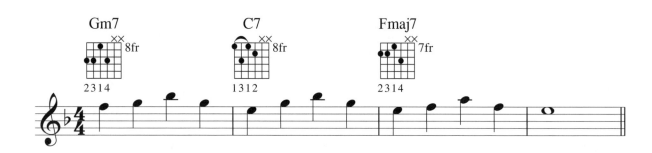

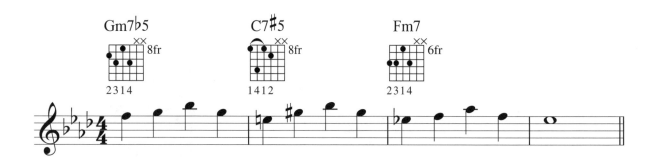

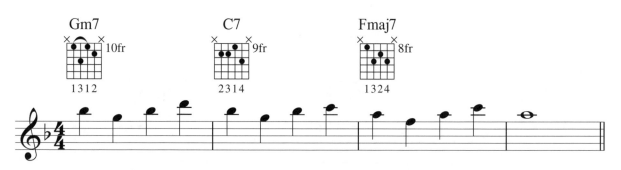

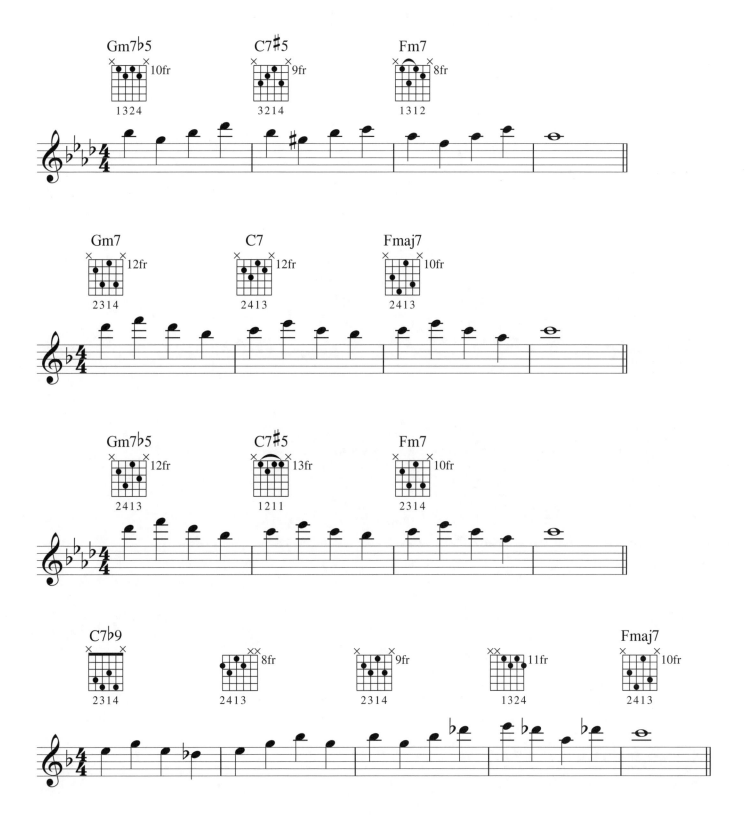

ii–V–I Drop 2 Diagonals Exercise in B♭

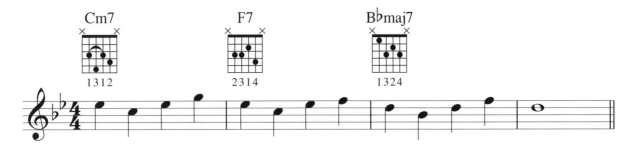

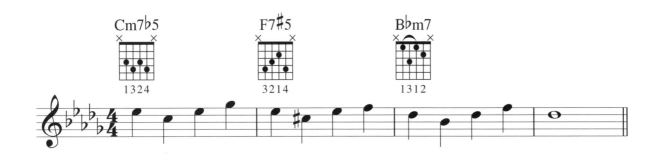

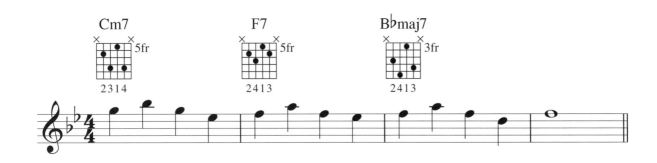

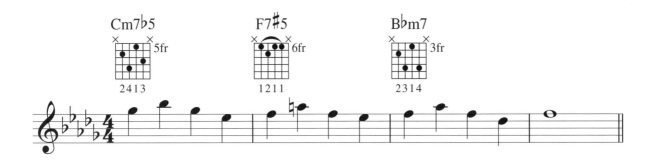

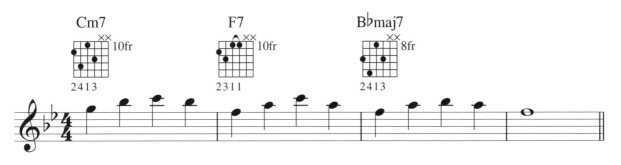

ii–V–I Drop 2 Diagonals Exercise in E♭

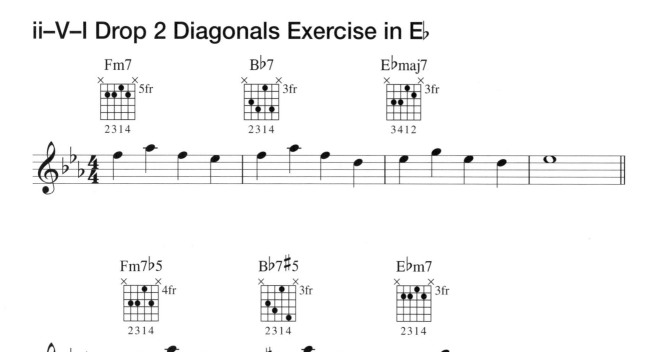

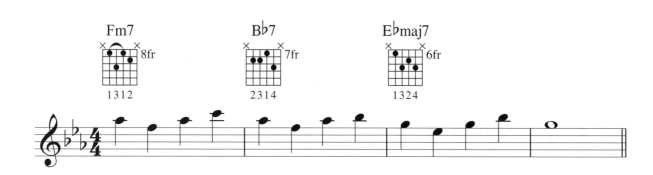

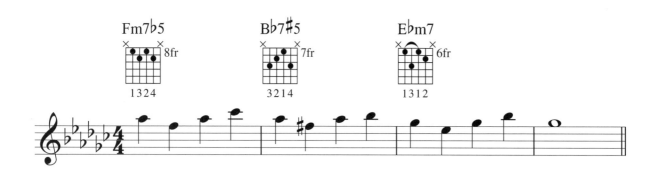

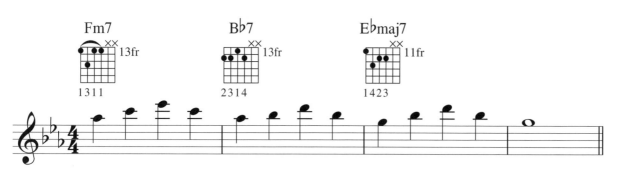

ii–V–I Drop 2 Diagonals Exercise in A♭

ii–V–I Drop 2 Diagonals Exercise in D♭/C♯

ii–V–I Drop 2 Diagonals Exercise in G♭/F♯

ii–V–I Drop 2 Diagonals Exercise in B

ii–V–I Drop 2 Diagonals Exercise in E

ii–V–I Drop 2 Diagonals Exercise in A

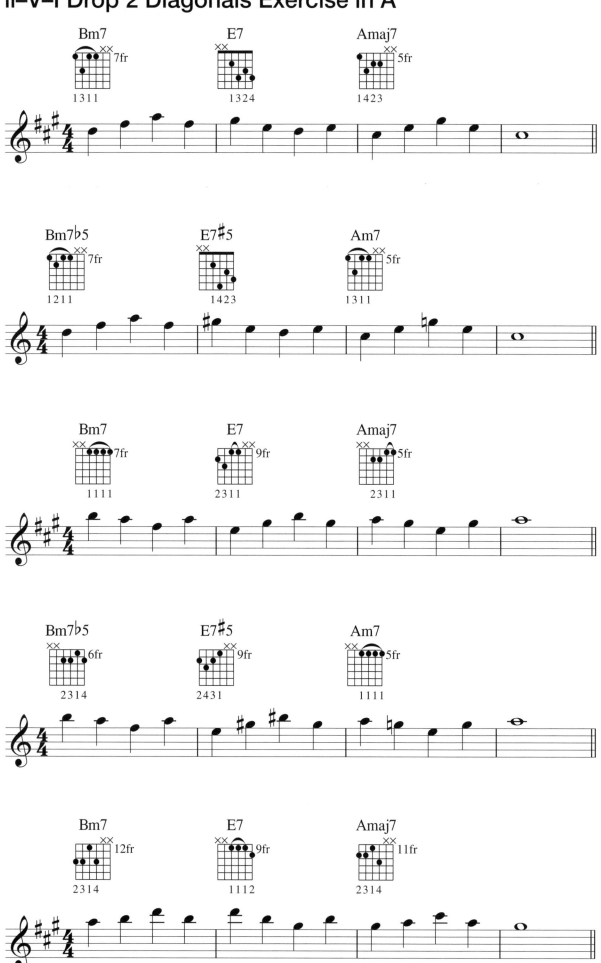

ii–V–I Drop 2 Diagonals Exercise in D

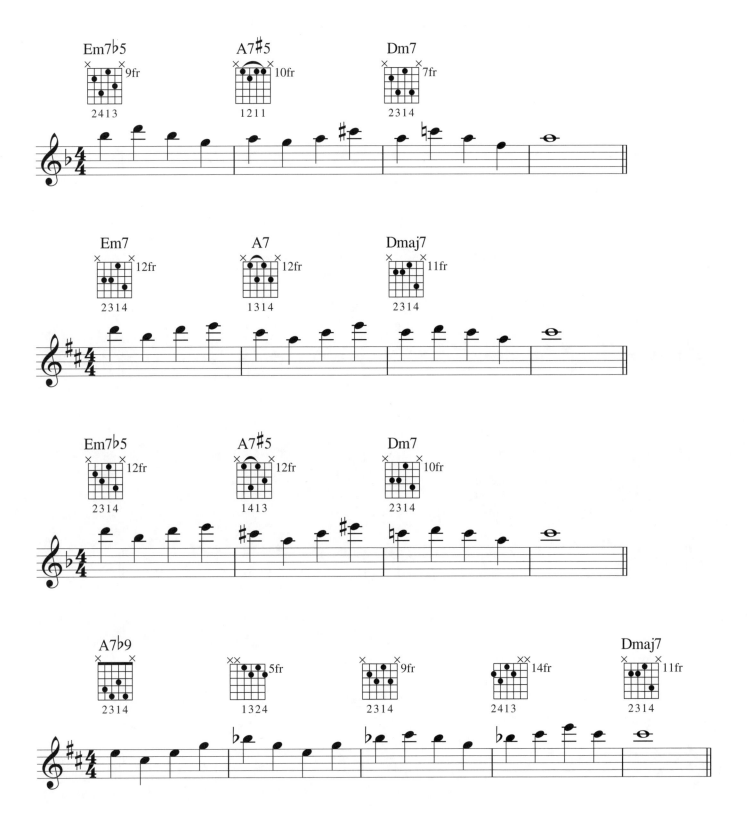

ii–V–I Drop 2 Diagonals Exercise in G

ii–V–I Drop 2 Diagonals Exercise in C

CHAPTER THREE

DROP 3 VOICINGS, LINEAR MOVEMENT

The next type of chord voicing we will learn is created using a very similar concept to Chapter 1. A *drop 3* voicing is created by lowering the second lowest voice of a standard closed voiced seventh chord by one octave.

These chords create a unique sound that puts some distance between the bass note and the rest of the chord.

STRING SET 5321

We'll start with the 5321 string set, learning the first set of chords—the qualities found in a major ii–V–I—by playing each one in F. Play each set of chords up and down the guitar while acclimating yourself with the fingerings, then add the following exercises to your one key per day routine.

Major ii–V–I Chords: m7, 7, maj7

Minor Seven

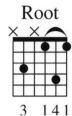
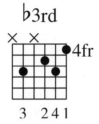
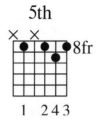
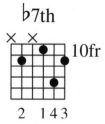

Dominant Seven

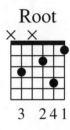
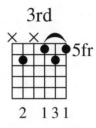
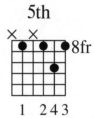
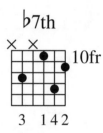

Major Seven

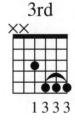
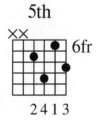
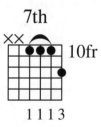

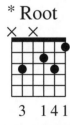

*You can substitute a
major sixth for
awkward stretches*

Major ii–V–I Exercise: String Set 5321

Minor ii–V–i Chords: m7♭5, 7, m7

As we did previously, let's explore what happens when we resolve to a minor chord. Again, the 5th is lowered on the ii chord and raised on the V chord. Play these voicings up and down the neck first as F chords until you are reasonably comfortable with the fingerings; then add the minor ii–V–i exercises to your one-key-per-day routine.

Minor Seven Flat Five

Root
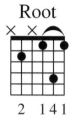
2 1 4 1

♭3rd
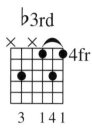
3 1 4 1

♭5th
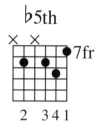
2 3 4 1

♭7th
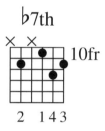
2 1 4 3

Augmented Seven

Root
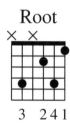
3 2 4 1

3rd
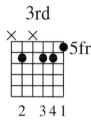
2 3 4 1

♯5th
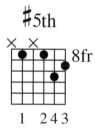
1 2 4 3

* ♭7th
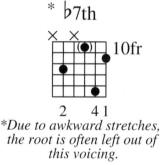
2   4 1

Due to awkward stretches, the root is often left out of this voicing.

Minor Seven

Root
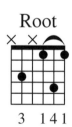
3 1 4 1

♭3rd
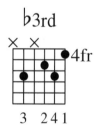
3 2 4 1

5th
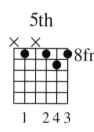
1 2 4 3

♭7th
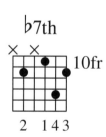
2 1 4 3

Minor ii–V–i Exercise: String Set 5321

Diminished Seventh Chords

As with our drop 2 diminished voicings, there is only one drop 3 fingering to learn for each set of strings.

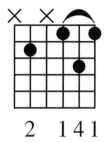

We will again explore the dual function of this chord, using it at a diminished passing chord or playing it a half step above the root to get a 7♭9 sound on the V chord.

Diminished Seventh Exercise: String Set 5321

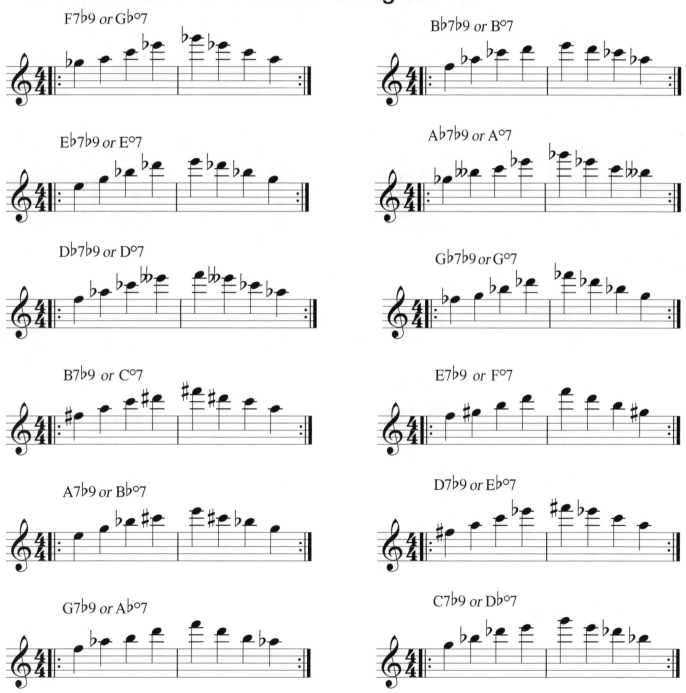

STRING SET 6432

To play our final set of drop 3 voicings, we will move them across one string set, putting the bass note on string 6. Practice the following C chords to absorb the new fingerings and then add the exercises to your one-key-per-day routine.

Major ii–V–I Chords: m7, 7, maj7

Minor Seven

 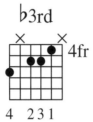 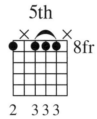 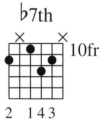

Root   ♭3rd   5th   ♭7th

3 141   4 231   2 333   2 143

Dominant Seven

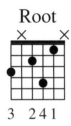 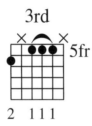 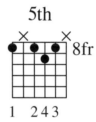 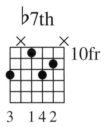

Root   3rd   5th   ♭7th

3 241   2 111   1 243   3 142

Major Seven

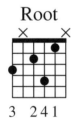 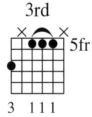 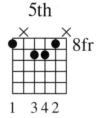 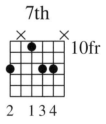

Root   3rd   5th   7th

3 241   3 111   1 342   2 134

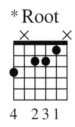

*Root

4 231

*Again, substitute
a major sixth
when applicable.

Major ii–V–I Exercise: String Set 6432

Minor ii–V–i Chords: m7♭5, 7♯5, m7

Apply the previous concepts to the minor ii-V-I chord set by learning the new fingerings as C chords first, then adding the following exercises to your one key per day practice routine.

Minor Seven Flat Five

 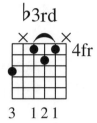 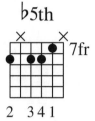 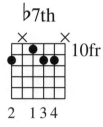

Augmented Seven

 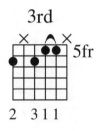 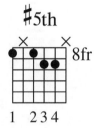 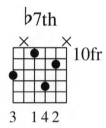

Minor Seven

 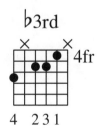 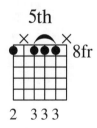 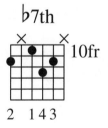

Minor ii–V–i Exercise: String Set 6432

Diminished Seventh Chords

Here's our one shape we need to learn for a drop 3 diminished seventh chord in the 6432 string set.

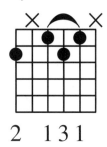

2 1 3 1

Diminished Seventh Chord Exercise: String Set 6432

F7♭9 *or* G♭°7

B♭7♭9 *or* B°7

E♭7♭9 *or* E°7

A♭7♭9 *or* A°7

D♭7♭9 *or* D°7

G♭7♭9 *or* G°7

B7♭9 *or* C°7

E7♭9 *or* F°7

A7♭9 *or* B♭°7

D7♭9 *or* E♭°7

G7♭9 *or* A♭°7

C7♭9 *or* D♭°7

CHAPTER FOUR

DROP 3 VOICINGS, DIAGONAL MOVEMENT

Now that you've had a chance to absorb the drop 3 fingerings in a linear fashion, we'll explore moving them across strings diagonally. Being that there are only two string sets, each diagonal line will consist of two chords. Practice the following frames to get your brain and fingers around these voicings with a D root first. Then proceed to adding the ii-V-I exercises to your one-key-per-day practice routine.

Diagonal Pattern Root–3rd

Dmaj7

Root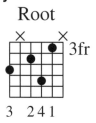

3rd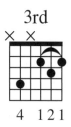

D7

Root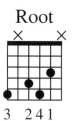

3rd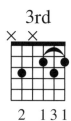

Dm7

Root

3rd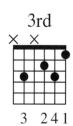

Dm7♭5

Root

3rd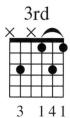

D7♯5

Root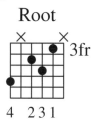

3rd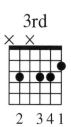

D♭7♭9/D°7

Root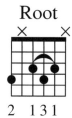

3rd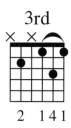

Diagonal Pattern 3rd–5th

Dmaj7

3rd
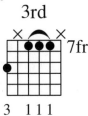
7fr
3 1 1 1

5th
5fr
1 3 4 2

D7

3rd
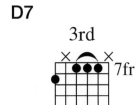
7fr
2 1 1 1

5th
5fr
1 2 4 3

Dm7

3rd
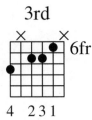
6fr
4 2 3 1

5th
5fr
1 2 4 3

Dm7♭5

3rd
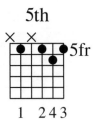
6fr
3 1 2 1

5th
4fr
2 3 4 1

D7♯5

3rd
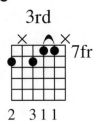
7fr
2 3 1 1

5th
5fr
1 2 4 3

D♭7♭9/D°7

3rd
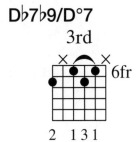
6fr
2 1 3 1

5th
4fr
2 1 4 1

Diagonal Pattern 5th–7th

Dmaj7

5th
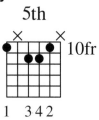
10fr

1 3 4 2

7th
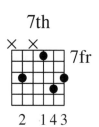
7fr

2 1 4 3

D7

5th
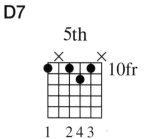
10fr

1 2 4 3

7th
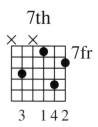
7fr

3 1 4 2

Dm7

5th
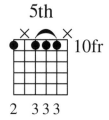
10fr

2 3 3 3

7th
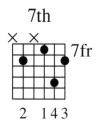
7fr

2 1 4 3

Dm7♭5

5th
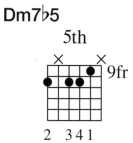
9fr

2 3 4 1

7th
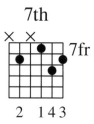
7fr

2 1 4 3

D7♯5

5th
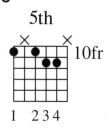
10fr

1 2 3 4

7th
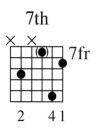
7fr

2 4 1

D♭7♭9/D°7

5th
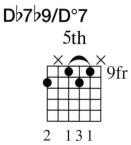
9fr

2 1 3 1

7th
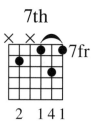
7fr

2 1 4 1

Diagonal Pattern 7th–Root

Dmaj7

7th   Root (D6)

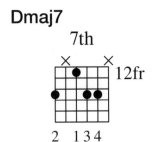
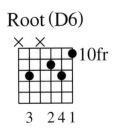

D7

7th   Root

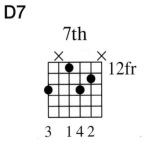
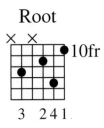

Dm7

7th   Root

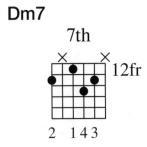
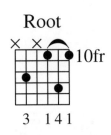

Dm7♭5

7th   Root

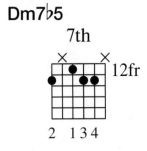
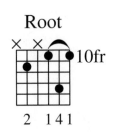

D7♯5

7th   Root

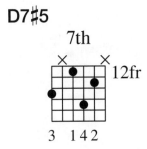
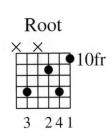

D♭7♭9/D°7

7th   Root

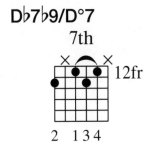
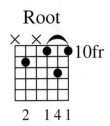

ii–V–I Drop 3 Diagonals Exercise in F

ii–V–I Drop 3 Diagonals Exercise in B♭

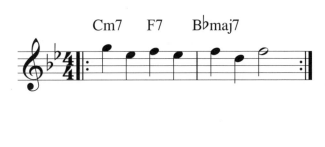

ii–V–I Drop 3 Diagonals Exercise in E♭

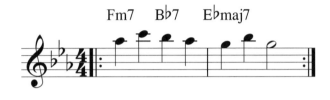

ii–V–I Drop 3 Diagonals Exercise in A♭/G♯

ii–V–I Drop 3 Diagonals Exercise in D♭/C♯

Ebm7 Ab7   Dbmaj7

D#m7b5 G#7#5   C#m7

Ebm7 Ab7   Dbmaj7

D#m7b5 G#7#5   C#m7

Ebm7 Ab7   Dbmaj7

D#m7b5 G#7#5   C#m7

Ebm7 Ab7   Dbmaj7

D#m7b5 G#7#5   C#m7

Ab7b9   Dbmaj7

ii–V–I Drop 3 Diagonals Exercise in G♭/F♯

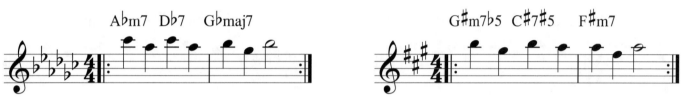

ii–V–I Drop 3 Diagonals Exercise in B

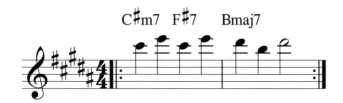

ii–V–I Drop 3 Diagonals Exercise in E

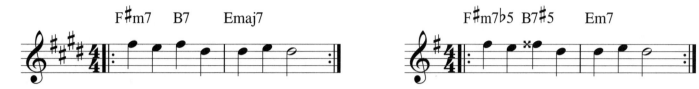

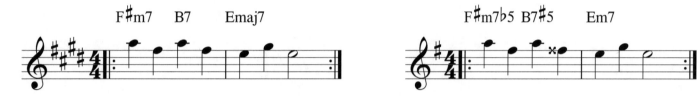

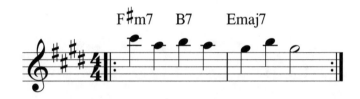

ii–V–I Drop 3 Diagonals Exercise in A

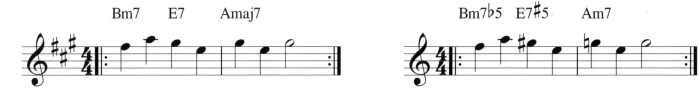

ii–V–I Drop 3 Diagonals Exercise in D

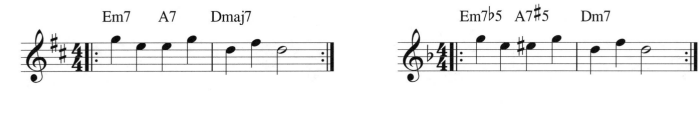

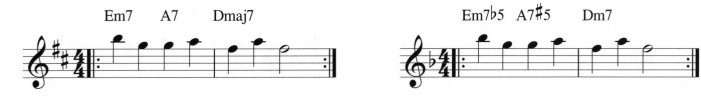

ii–V–I Drop 3 Diagonals Exercise in G

ii–V–I Drop 3 Diagonals Exercise in C

CHAPTER FIVE

ii–V–I MELODIC PATTERNS

The goal of this chapter is to explore the multitude of ways one can resolve a major or minor ii–V–I progression in regards to how the highest voice of the chord leads into the next. As you will notice, only chord frames are used to enable playing these exercises in your "key of the day." Play a different page everyday in a different key.

The student must manually put each chord frame on the correct fret, depending on the key chosen. For example, let's look at our first exercise: ii–V–I Melodic Pattern Root–Fifth–Root. If your key of the day is F, your task is to play ii as Gm7, V as C7, and I as Fmaj7. The first chord frames shown for string group 4321 would then be Gm7 on fret 3, C7 on fret 1, and Fmaj7 on fret 1. If your key of the day happened to be B♭, the same chord frames would be Cm7 on fret 8, F7 on fret 6, and B♭maj7 on fret 6. Practicing this way enables each melodic pattern to be played in all 12 keys while cementing which notes are ii, V, and I in the given key. Try saying the names of each chord as you play the exercise.

These exercises start with intervals that are as close to each other as possible and then branch out to wider interval jumps. As the intervals grow wider, the "Across Strings" patterns become more practical. The idea is to continually expose yourself to each of these resolutions in a "little by little," daily practice kind of way, allowing them to naturally seep in to your chordal vocabulary. For added fun, try changing the im7 to a im(maj7) in the minor ii–Vs.

Melodic Pattern Root–5th–Root

The ii and V stay as close as possible and then resolve downward to the I chord.

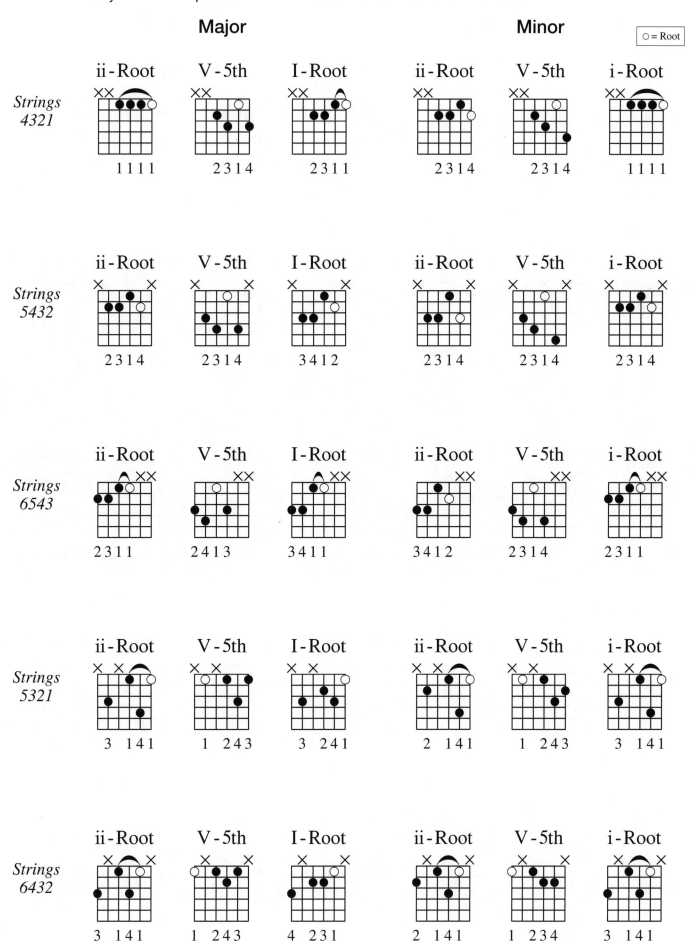

Melodic Pattern 3rd–7th–3rd

The ii and V stay as close as possible and then resolve downward to the I chord.

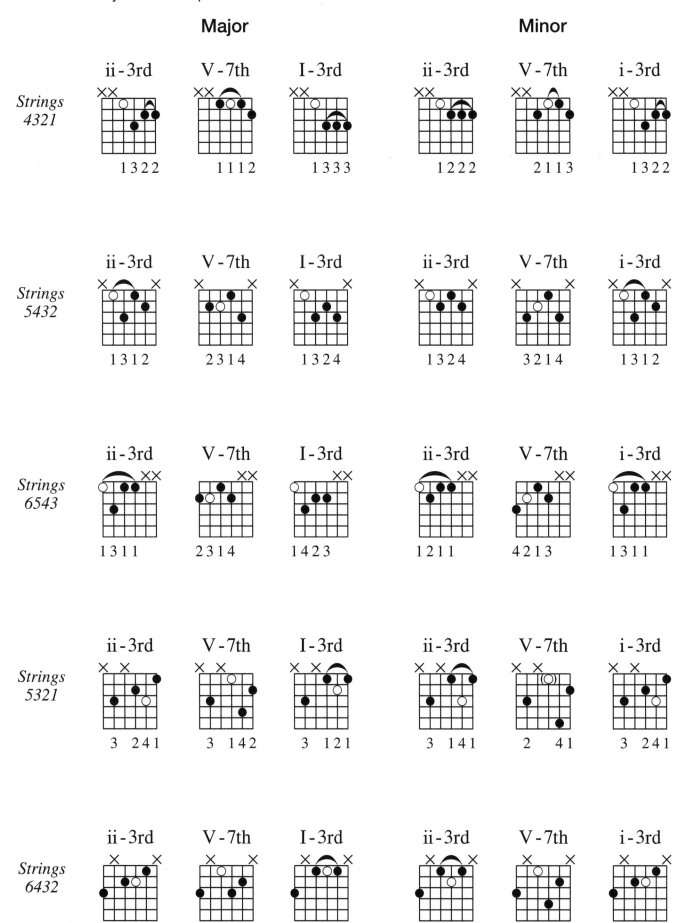

Melodic Pattern 5th–Root–5th

The ii resolves downward to V and stays as close as possible to the I.

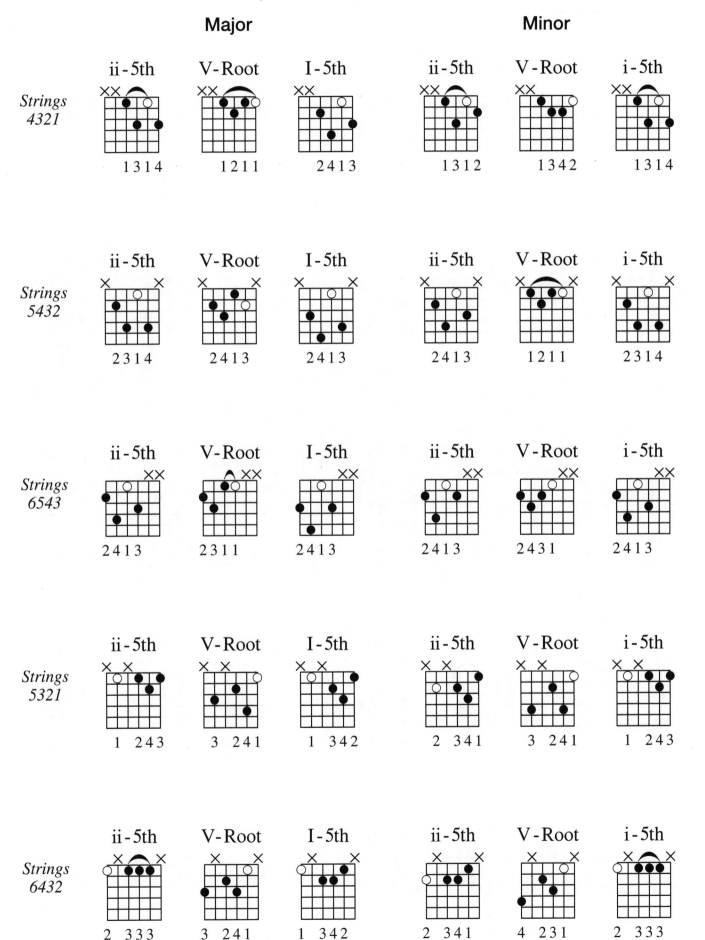

Melodic Pattern 7th–3rd–7th

The ii resolves downward to V and stays as close as possible to the I.

	Major			**Minor**	

Strings 4321

ii - 7th   V - 3rd   I - 7th   ii - 7th   V - 3rd   i - 7th

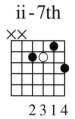 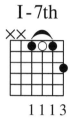 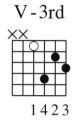

2 3 1 4   1 3 2 4   1 1 1 3   1 3 2 4   1 4 2 3   2 3 1 4

Strings 5432

ii - 7th   V - 3rd   I - 7th   ii - 7th   V - 3rd   i - 7th

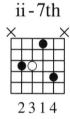 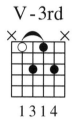 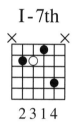 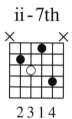 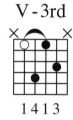 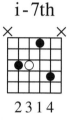

2 3 1 4   1 3 1 4   2 3 1 4   2 3 1 4   1 4 1 3   2 3 1 4

Strings 6543

ii - 7th   V - 3rd   I - 7th   ii - 7th   V - 3rd   i - 7th

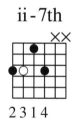 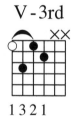 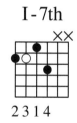 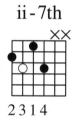 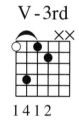 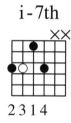

2 3 1 4   1 3 2 1   2 3 1 4   2 3 1 4   1 4 1 2   2 3 1 4

Strings 5321

ii - 7th   V - 3rd   I - 7th   ii - 7th   V - 3rd   i - 7th

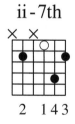 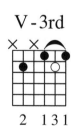 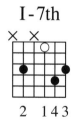 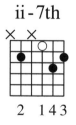 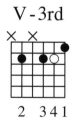 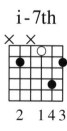

2   1 4 3   2   1 3 1   2   1 4 3   2   1 4 3   2   3 4 1   2   1 4 3

Strings 6432

ii - 7th   V - 3rd   I - 7th   ii - 7th   V - 3rd   i - 7th

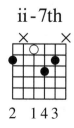 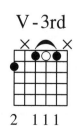 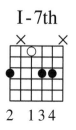 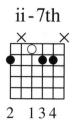 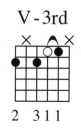 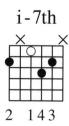

2   1 4 3   2   1 1 1   2   1 3 4   2   1 3 4   2   3 1 1   2   1 4 3

Melodic Pattern 7th–3rd–Root

The ii moves downward to the V and then back upward to the I.

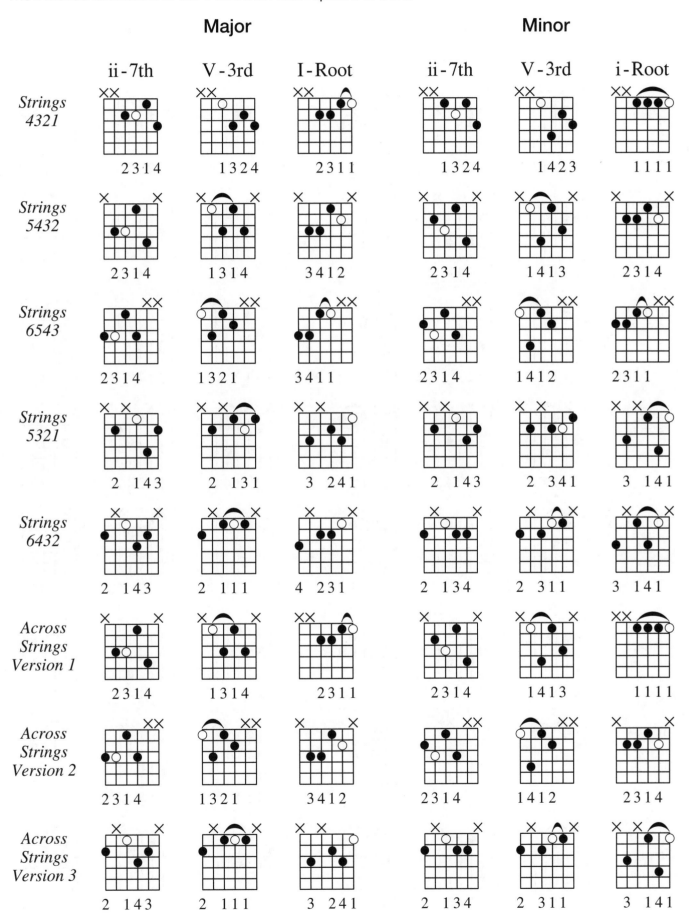

Melodic Pattern Root–5th–3rd

The ii and V stay as close as possible and then resolve upward to the I.

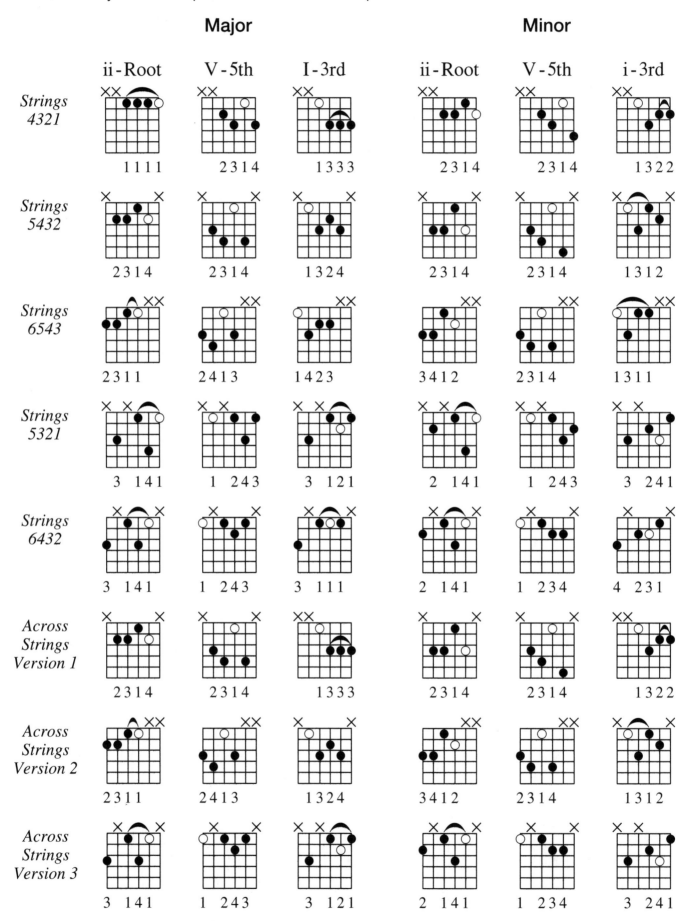

Melodic Pattern 3rd–7th–5th

The ii stays as close as possible to the V and resolves upward to the I.

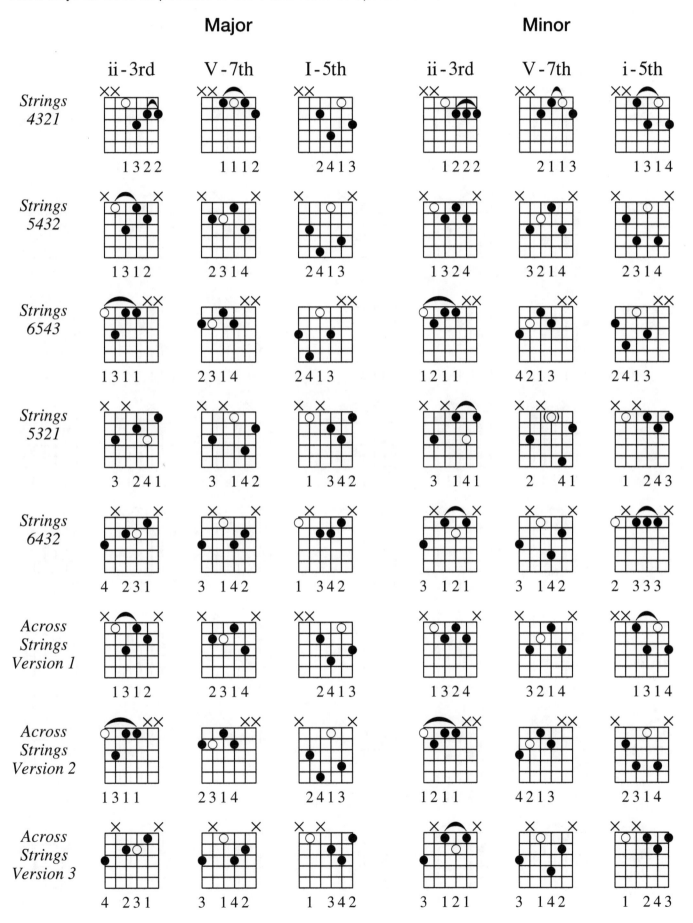

Melodic Pattern 5th–3rd–7th

The ii resolves upward to the V and stays as close as possible to the I.

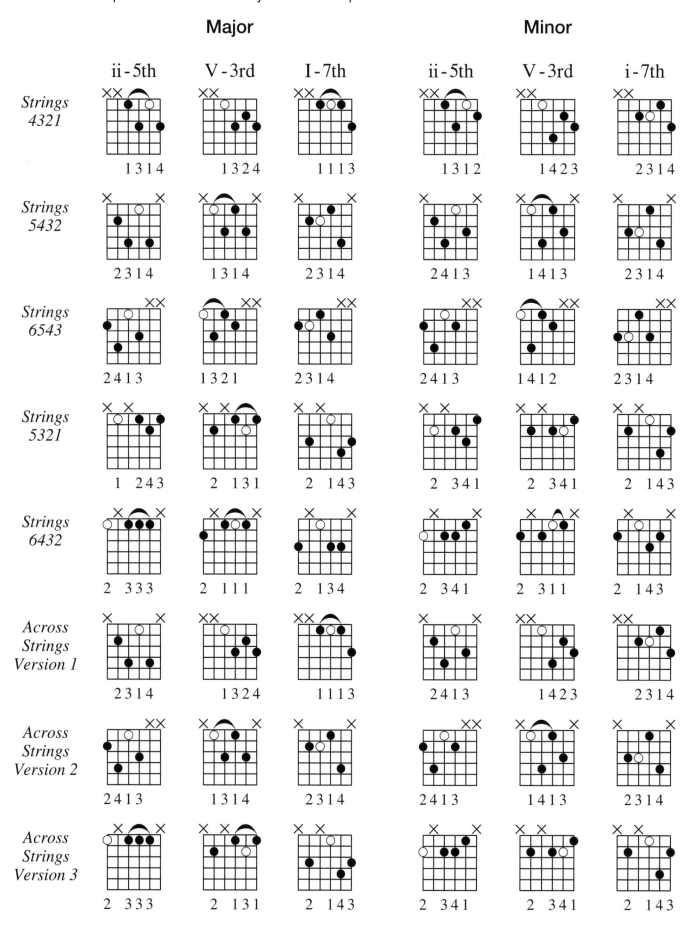

Melodic Pattern 7th–5th–Root

The ii moves upward to V and then resolves downward to the I.

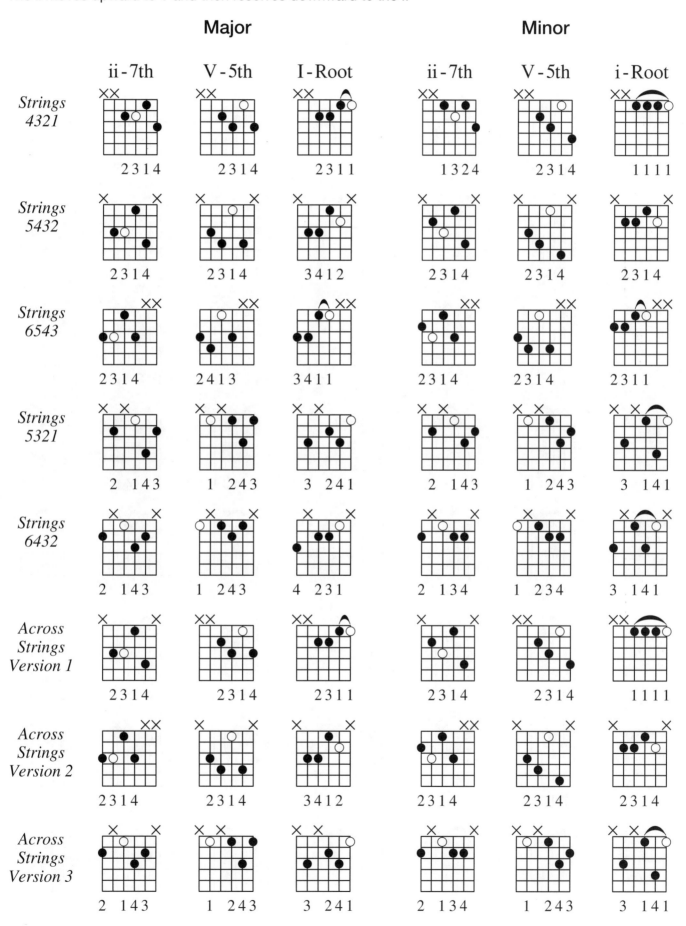

Melodic Pattern Root–3rd–Root

The ii moves downward to V and then back up to the I.

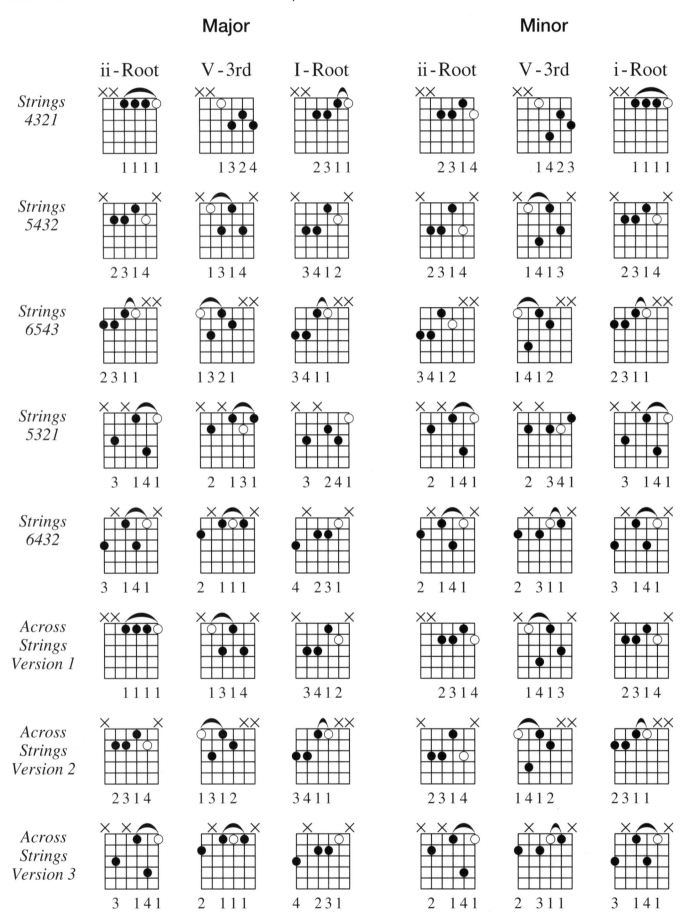

Melodic Pattern 3rd–5th–3rd

The ii moves downward to V and then resolves upward to the I.

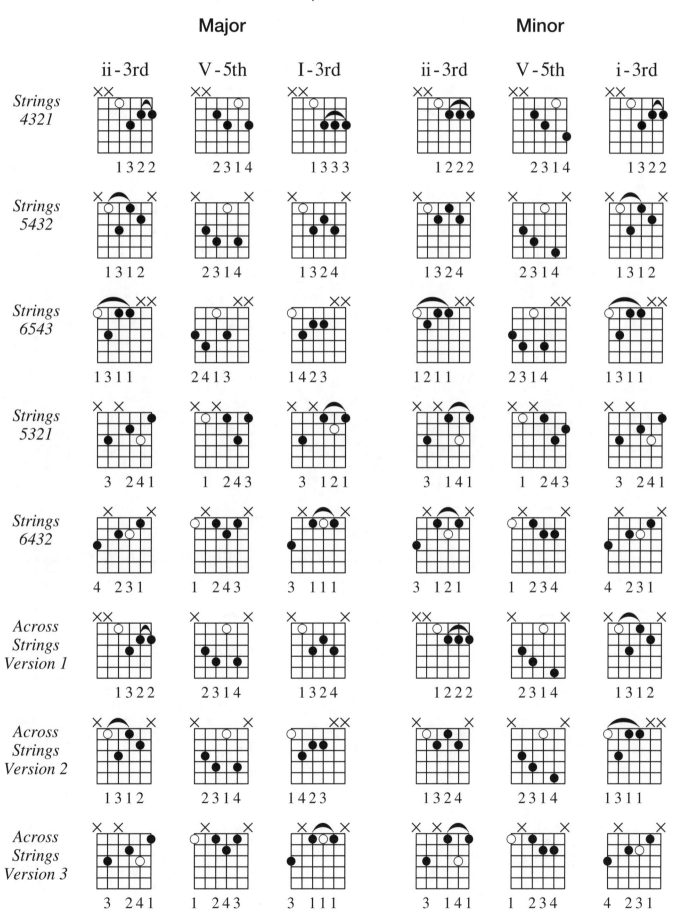

Melodic Pattern 5th–7th–5th

The ii moves downward to V and then resolves upward to the I.

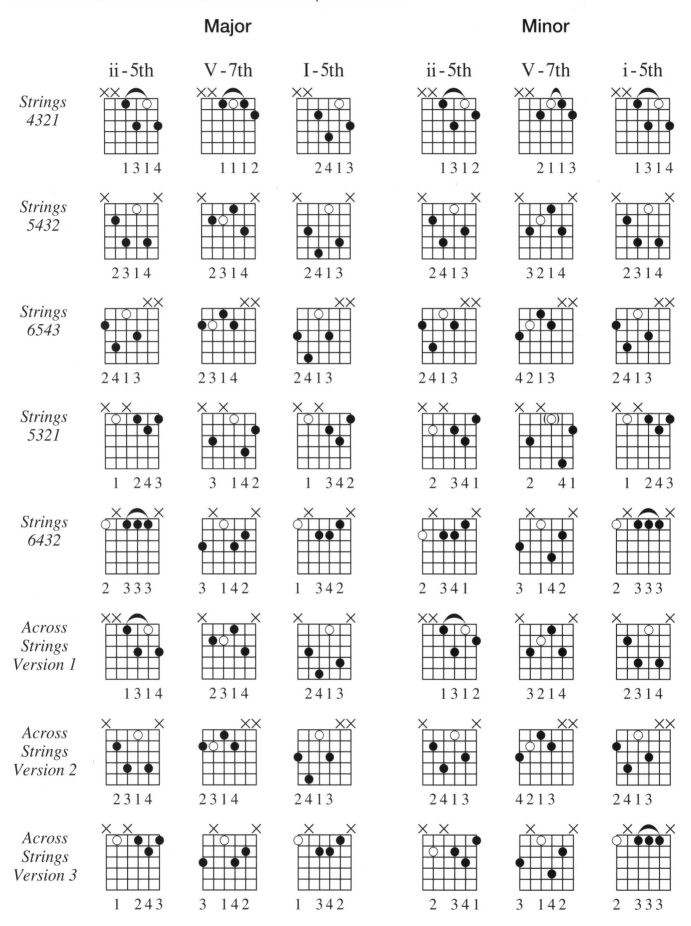

Melodic Pattern 7th–Root–7th

The ii moves downward to V and then upward to the I.

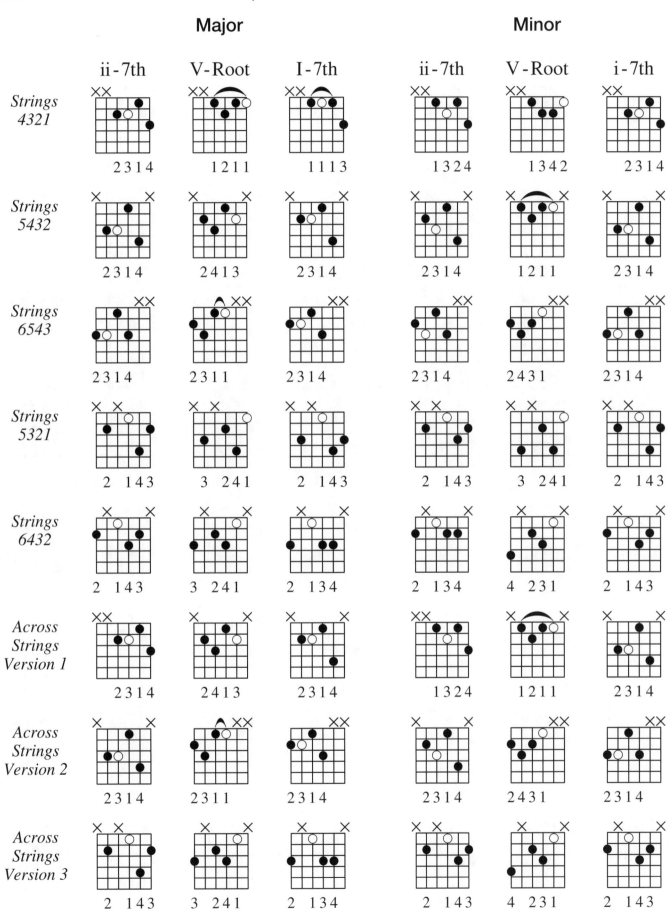

Melodic Pattern Root–7th–3rd

The ii moves upward to V and then resolves downward to the I.

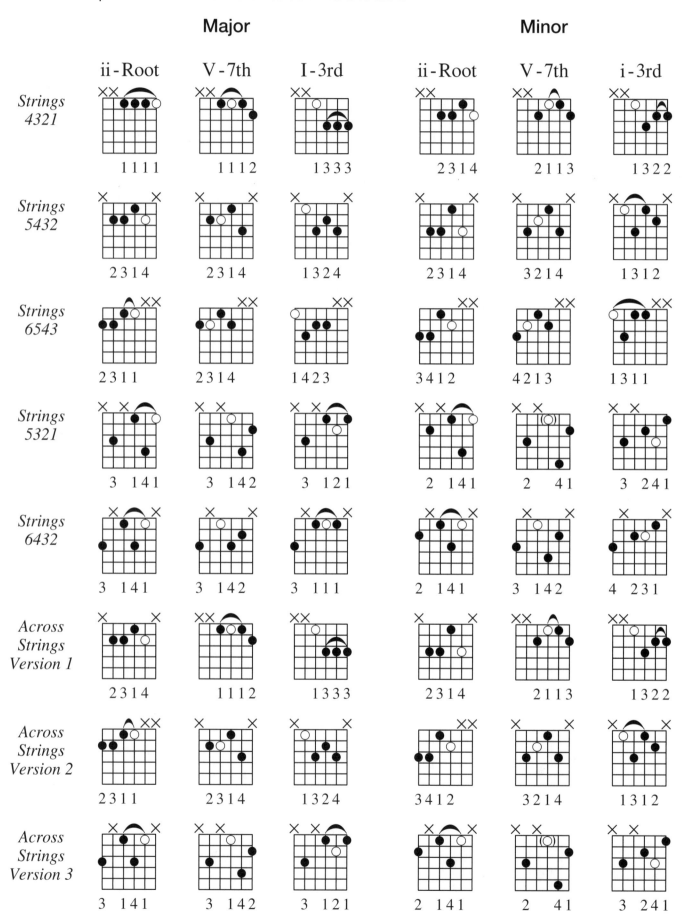

Melodic Pattern 3rd–Root–5th

The ii moves upward to V and then stays as close as possible to I.

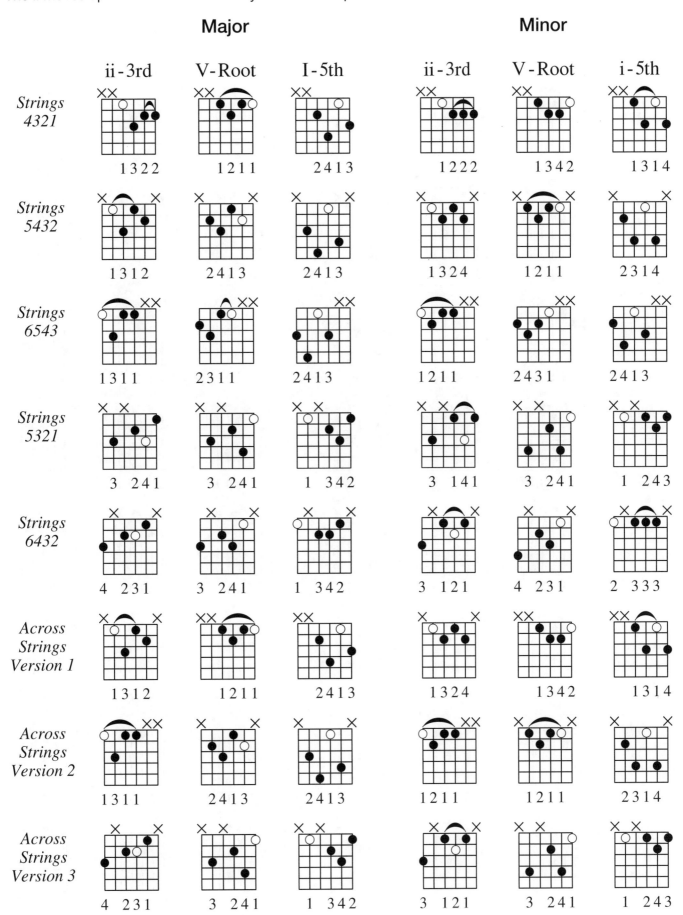

Melodic Pattern Root–3rd–5th

The chords descend linearly without repeating notes.

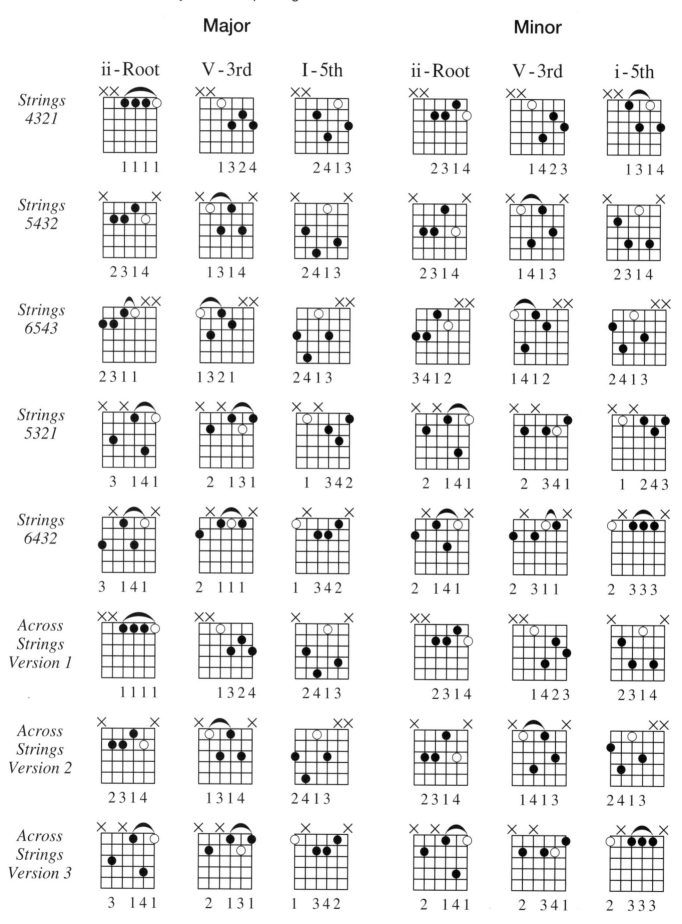

Melodic Pattern 3rd–5th–Root

The chords descend linearly without repeating notes.

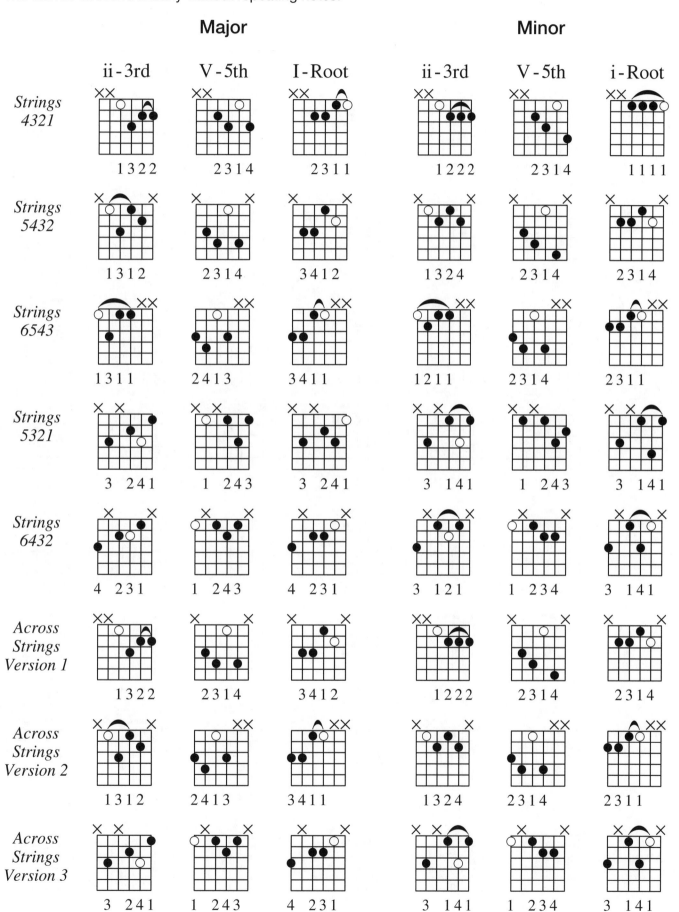

Melodic Pattern 5th–Root–3rd

The chords descend linearly without repeating notes.

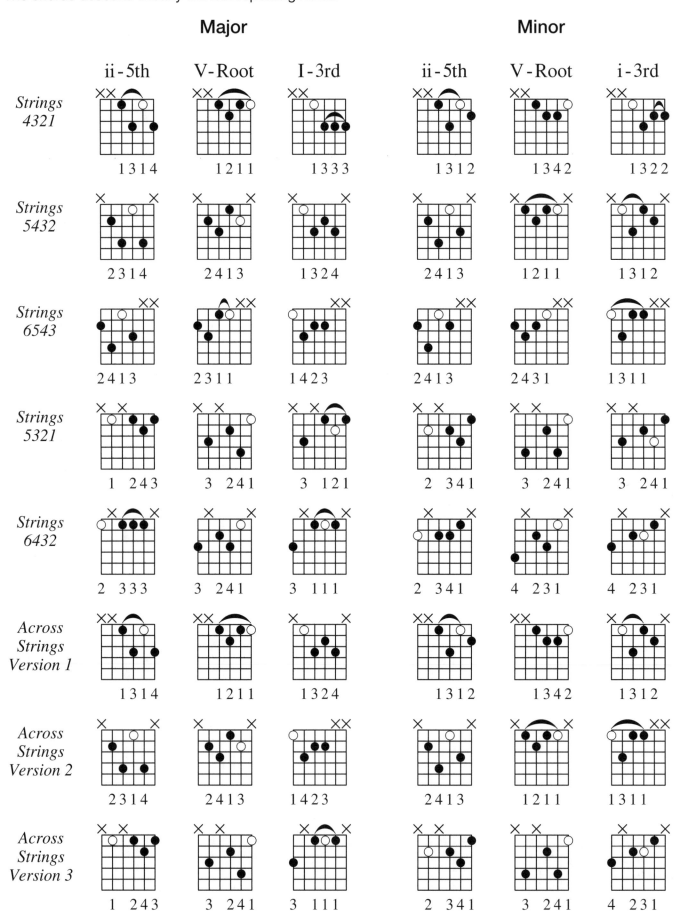

Melodic Pattern 7th–3rd–5th

The chords descend linearly without repeating notes.

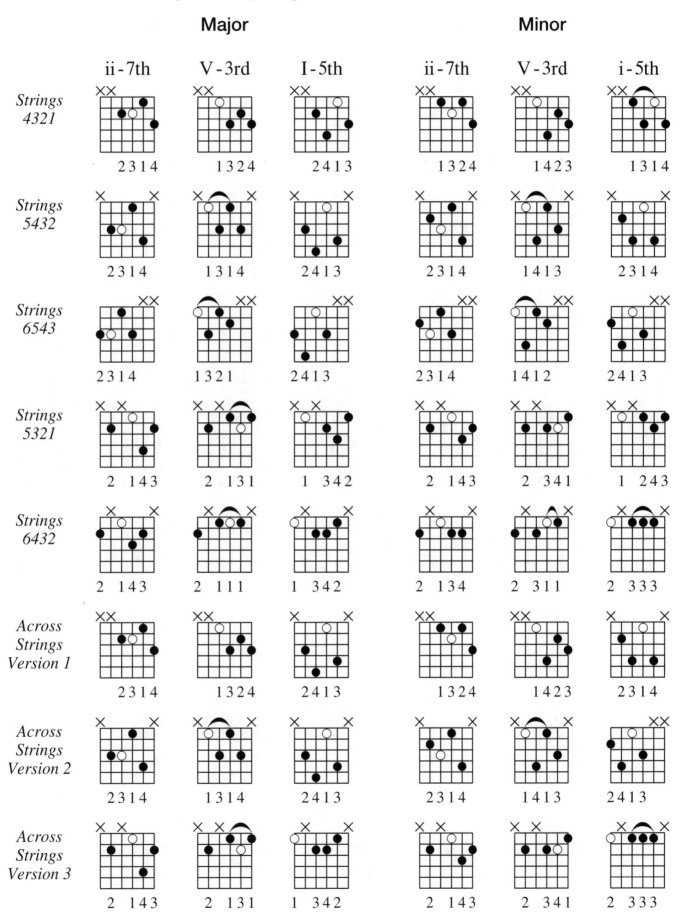

Melodic Pattern Root–7th–5th

The chords ascend linearly without repeating notes.

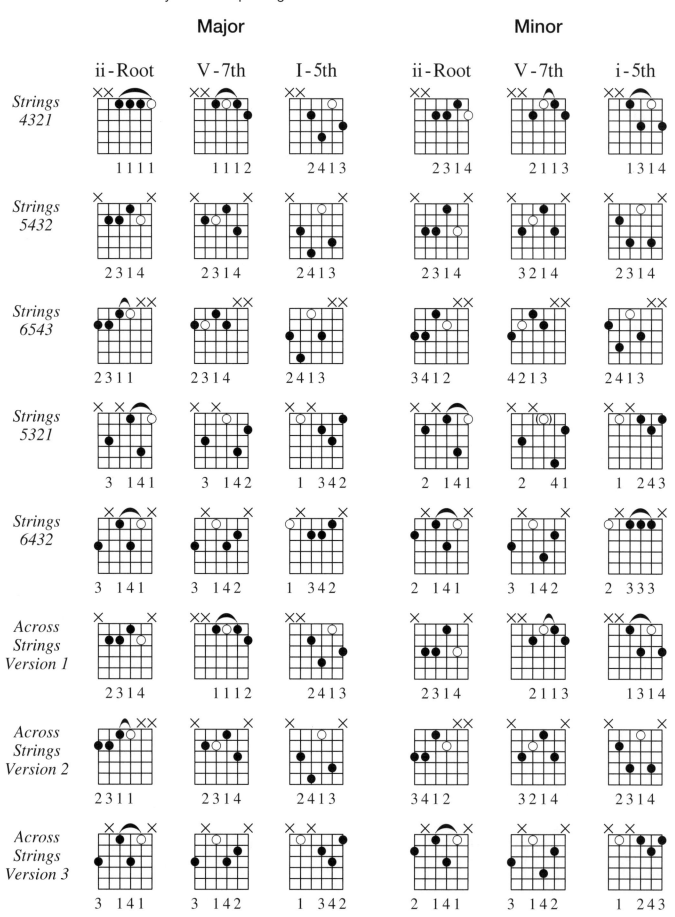

Melodic Pattern 3rd–Root–7th

The chords ascend linearly without repeating notes.

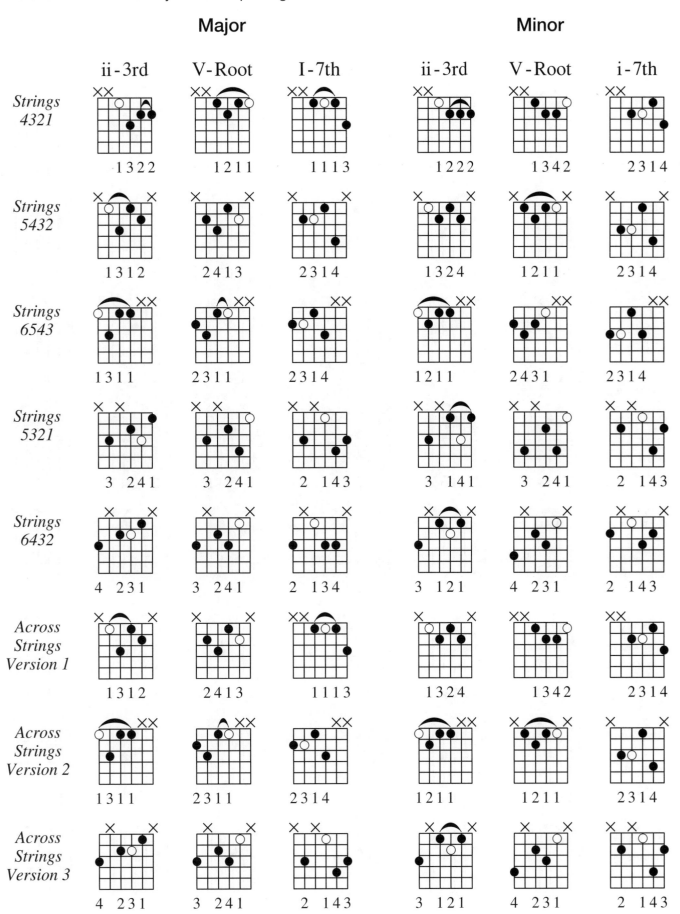

Melodic Pattern 5th–3rd–Root

The chords ascend linearly without repeating notes.

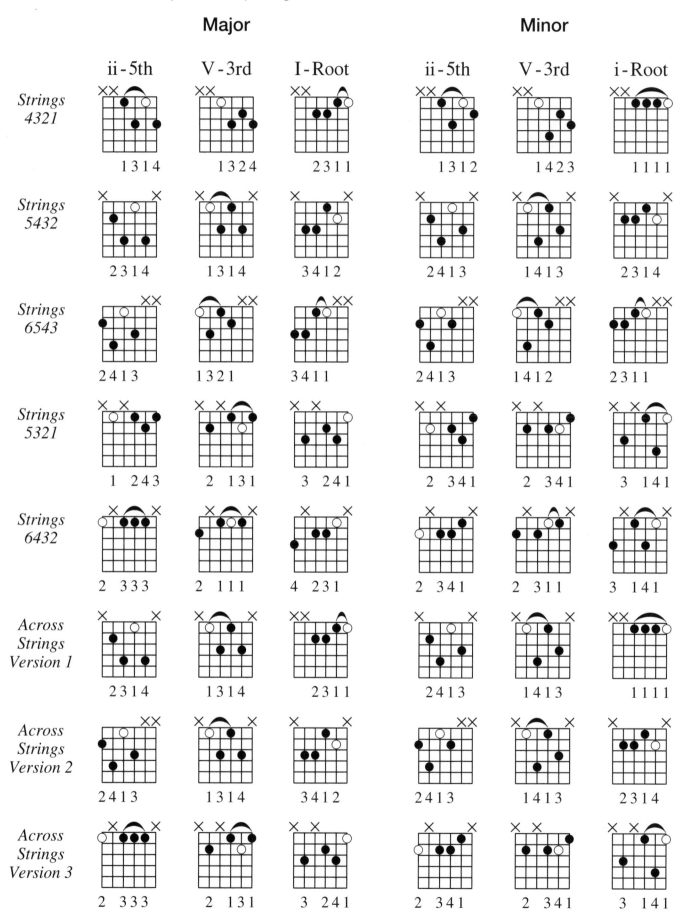

Melodic Pattern 7th–5th–3rd

The chords ascend linearly without repeating notes.

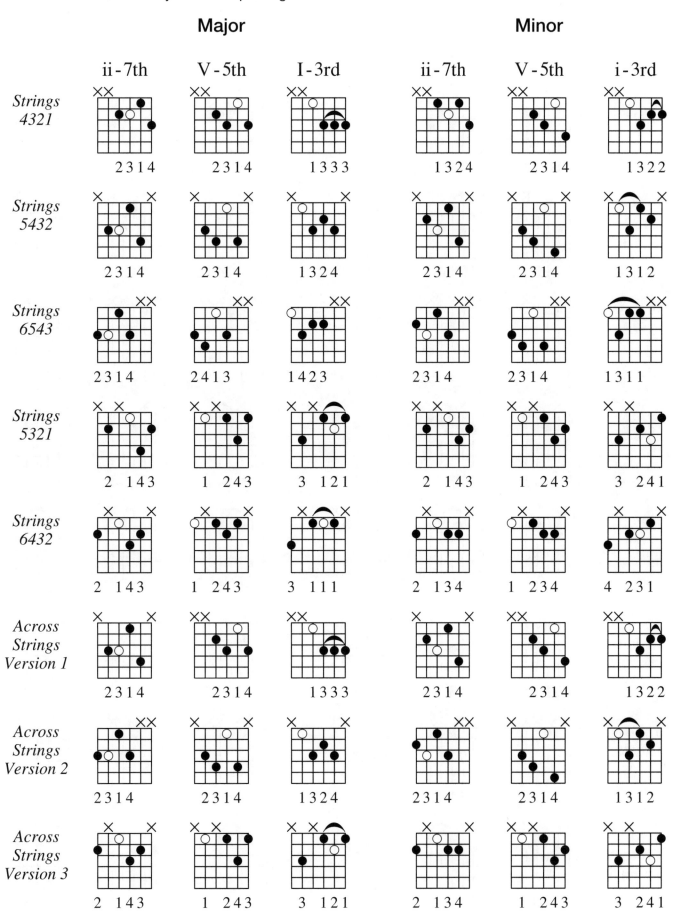

Melodic Pattern 3rd–3rd–5th

This uses wider intervals; the ii moves upward to V and then resolves downward to I.

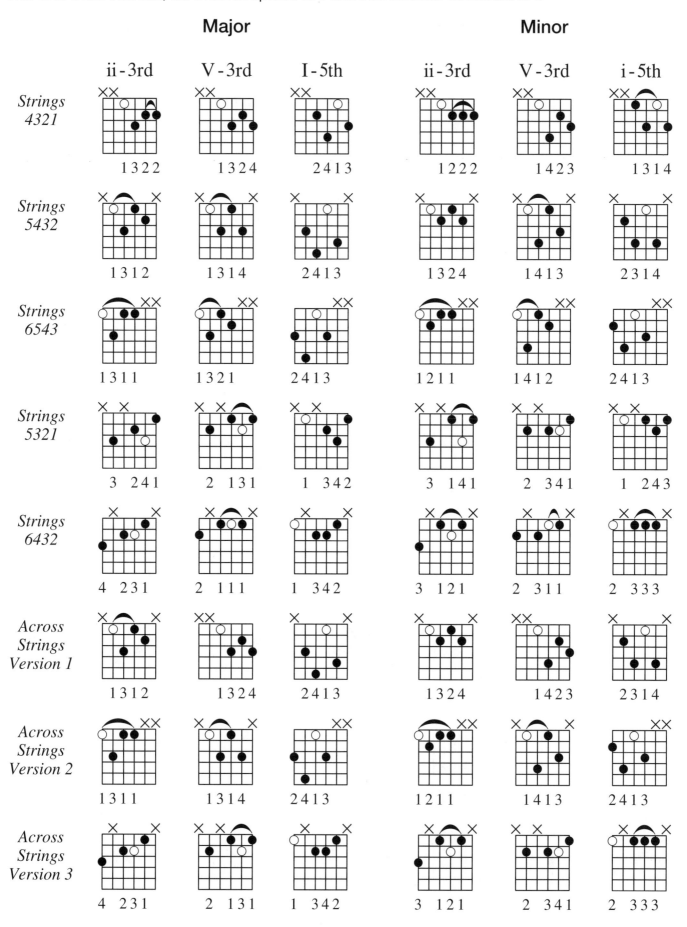

Melodic Pattern 5th–5th–Root

This uses wider intervals; the ii moves upward to V and then resolves downward to I.

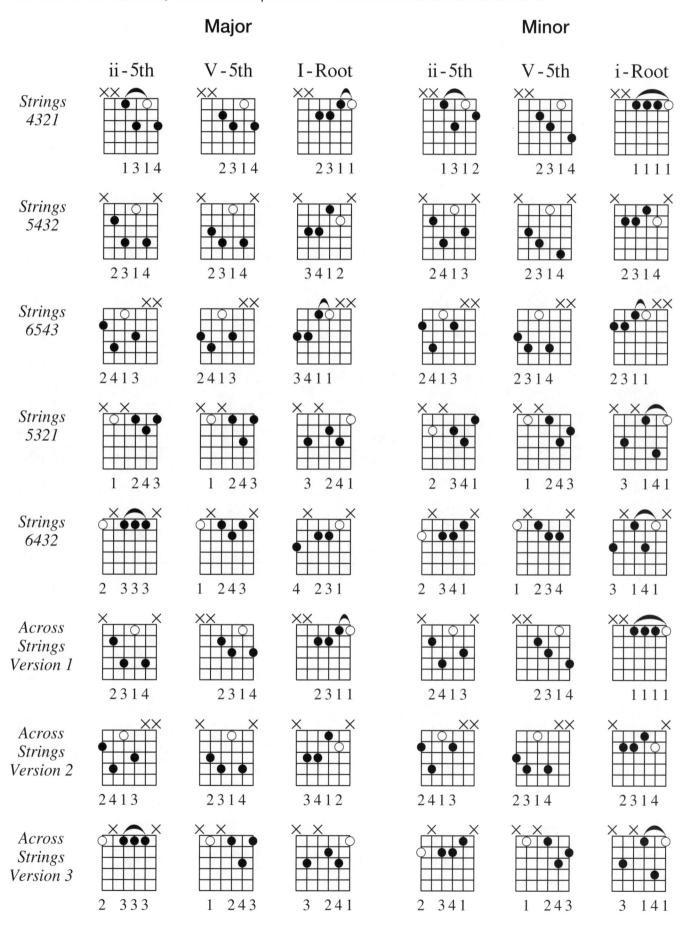

Melodic Pattern 5th–5th–7th

This uses wider intervals; the ii moves upward to V and then resolves downward to I.

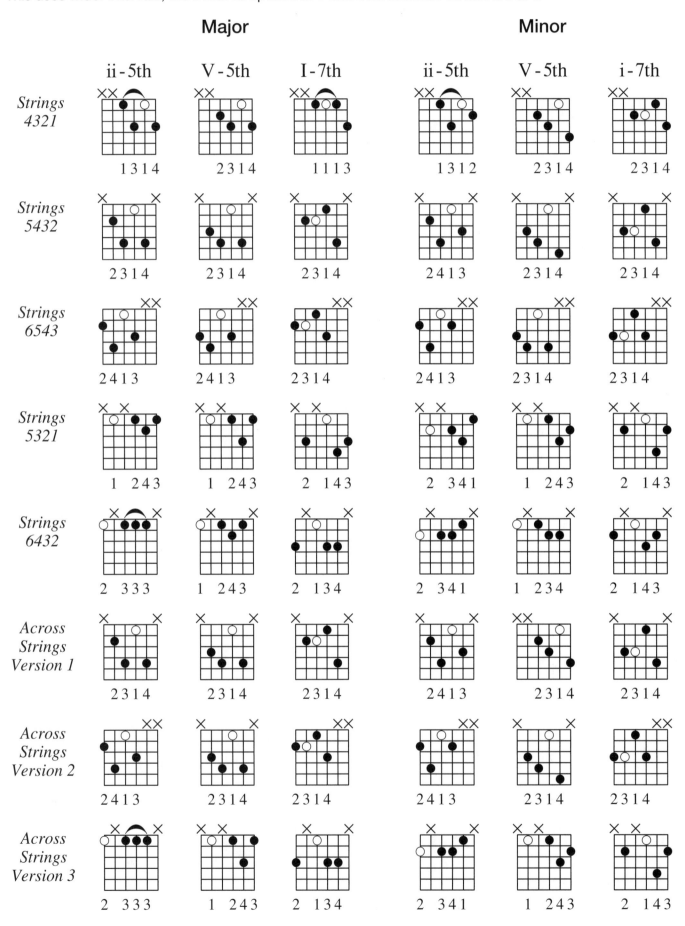

Melodic Pattern 7th–7th–3rd

This uses wider intervals; the ii moves upward to V and then resolves downward to I.

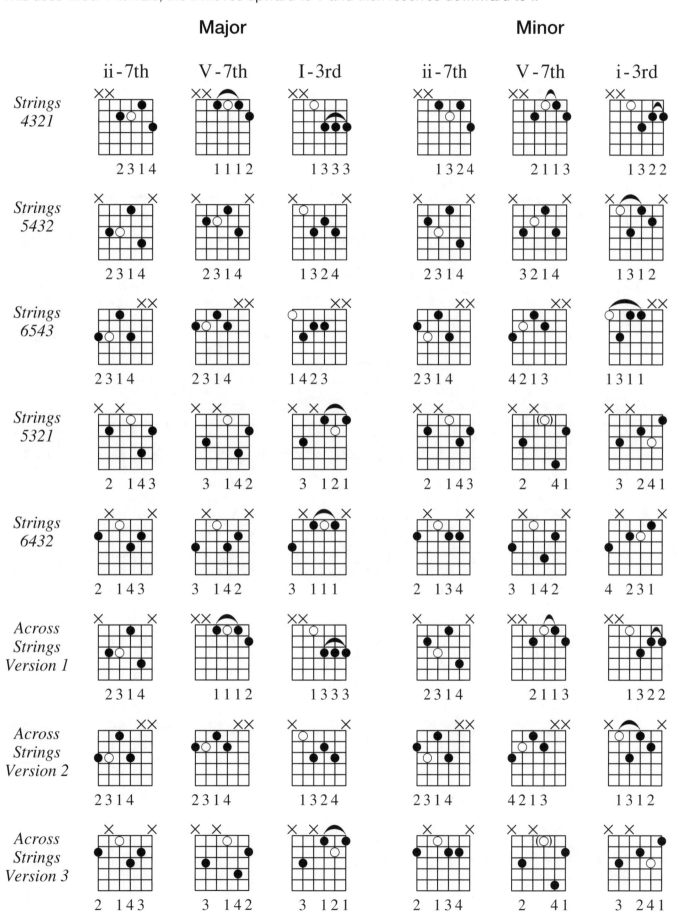

Melodic Pattern Root–Root–7th

This uses wider intervals; the ii moves downward to V and then resolves upward to I.

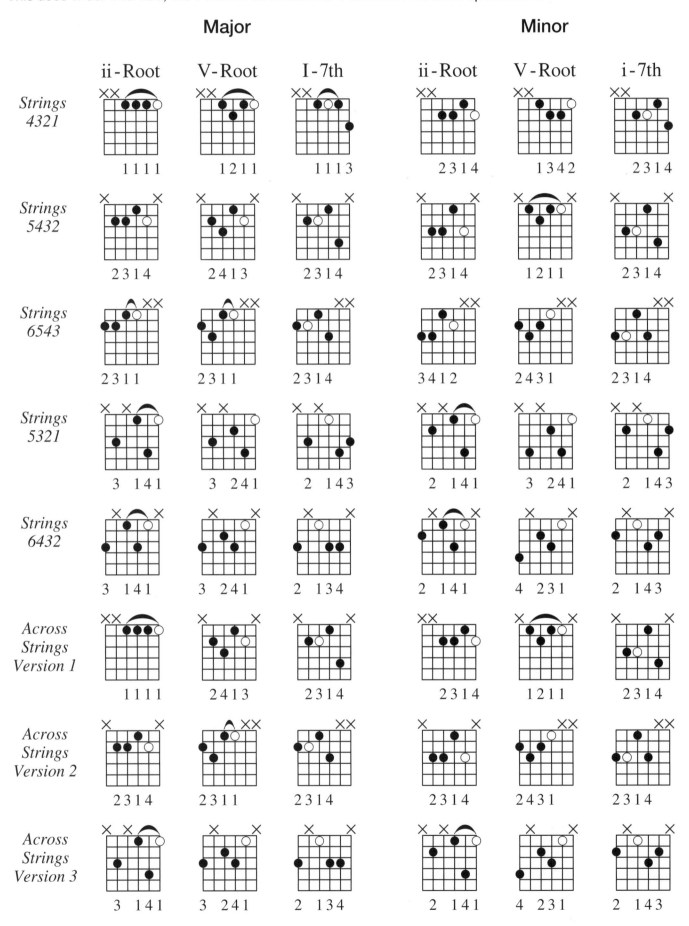

Melodic Pattern Root–Root–3rd

This uses wider intervals; the ii moves upward to V and then resolves downward to I.

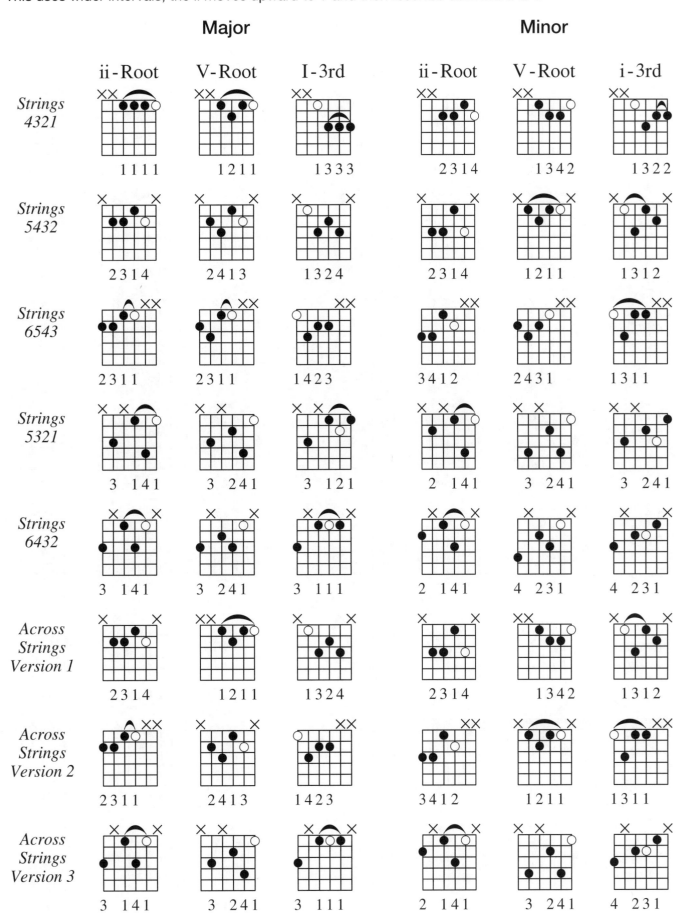

Melodic Pattern 3rd–3rd–Root

This uses wider intervals; the ii moves downward to V and then resolves upward to I.

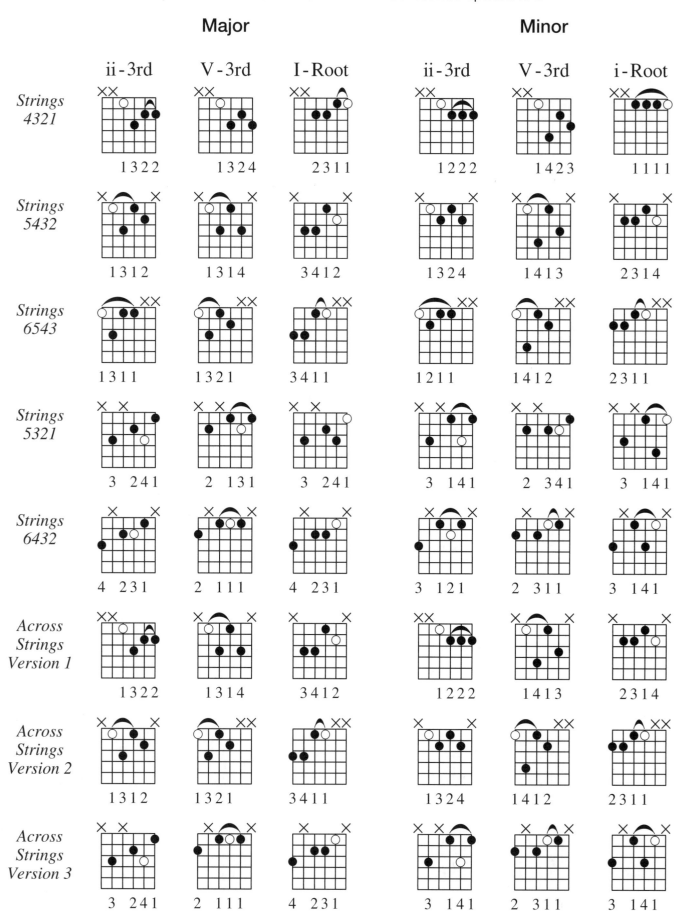

Melodic Pattern 5th–5th–3rd

This uses wider intervals; the ii moves downward to V and then resolves upward to I.

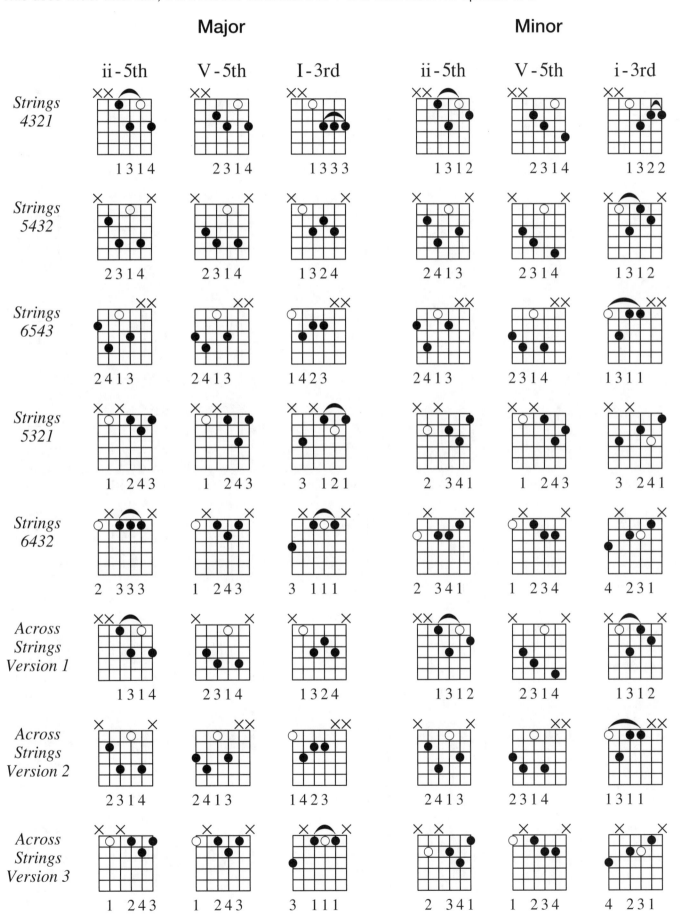

Melodic Pattern 7th–7th–5th

This uses wider intervals; the ii moves downward to V and then resolves upward to I.

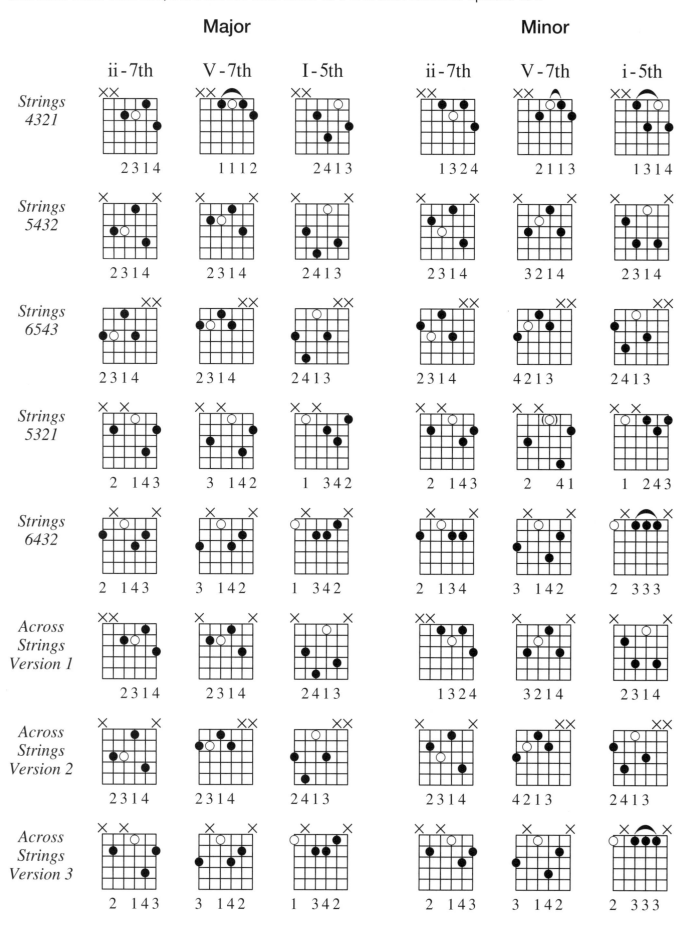

CHAPTER SIX

APPLYING YOUR NEW CHORDS

As with any new tool you put in your toolbox, the final step is to apply it to some actual music. The following arrangements focus on using the voicings and devices presented in the previous chapters and suggest ways to incorporate them with the chords you already use. The first six arrangements concentrate on using either drop 2 or drop 3 voicings specifically, allowing one to focus on each type of chord. The final four explore some of the voice leading possibilities available when both sets of chords are combined. For most of the songs, there are three audio tracks. The first one is a slow demo that presents the song exactly as written, while the second one is a full-speed version that first presents the chords written and then provides several choruses (a "chorus" is one time through the form) of chordal improvisation. The third track is a full-speed version minus the guitar. (The slower ballads, such as "My One and Only Love," contain two tracks only: the normal speed, with improvisation in subsequent choruses, and the minus-guitar version.)

Additionally, two new concepts are presented in "Straight No Chaser" and "Corcavado" that bear mentioning: *ninth chords* and *minor sixth chords*.

Ninth Chords

One way to get extra mileage from fingerings you already know can be accomplished by simply changing one note of a chord. In the case of our dominant sevenths, it is common practice to change the root of the chord to the 9th by moving it up two frets. Doing so instantly provides a new set of rootless dominant chords, which you'll realize are the exact same fingerings as our minor 7♭5 chord sets. This idea is explored throughout "Straight No Chaser." One way you may associate this idea is to realize that the fingerings for B♭9 and Dm7♭5 are the same, or that a dominant ninth chord shares the fingering of a m7♭5 chord a major 3rd higher.

Minor Sixth Chords

In the same way we modified a dominant seventh chord by moving one note, we can generate a set of minor sixth chords by simply lowering the ♭7th of a minor seventh chord a half step to the 6th. By doing so, you will find that the new chord shares the exact same fingering as a m7♭5 chord played down a minor 3rd. For example, Am6 chords share the same fingering as F#m7♭5 chords. This concept is explored in "Corcavado."

Play the following examples and listen to the recordings for more ideas on how to use your new chord voicings. The recordings are longer than the written music, for additional play-along time. Then have fun creating your own ways to use the multitude of chords available to you. Good luck!

Autumn Leaves

Track 1: Slow Demo
Track 2: Full Speed
Track 3: Full Speed (minus guitar)

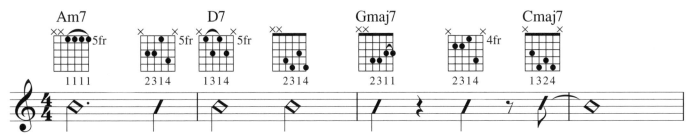

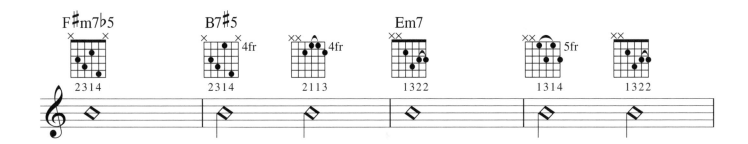

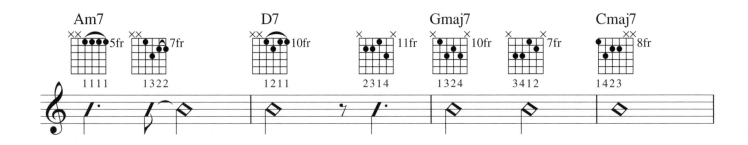

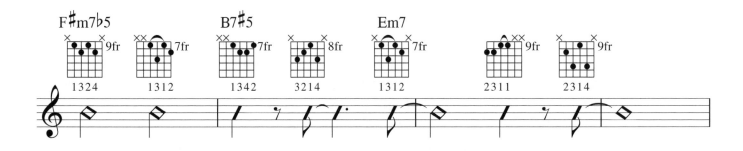

All the Things You Are

Track 4: Slow Demo
Track 5: Full Speed
Track 6: Full Speed (minus guitar)

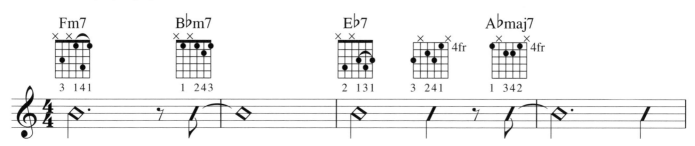

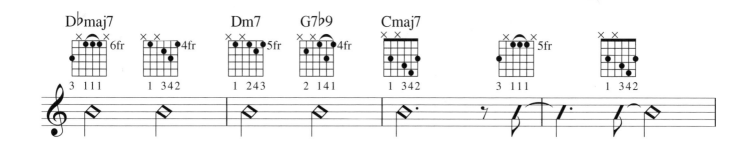

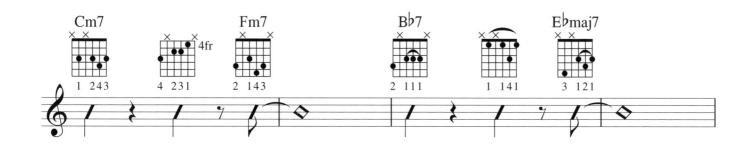

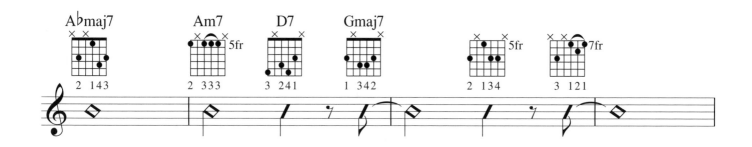

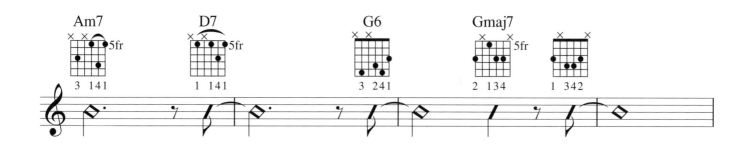

My One and Only Love

Track 7: Full Speed
Track 8: Full Speed (minus guitar)

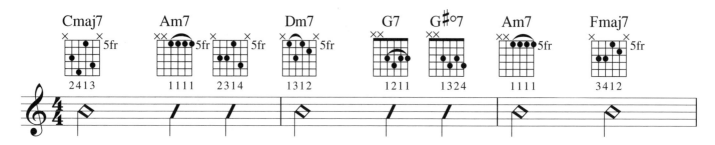

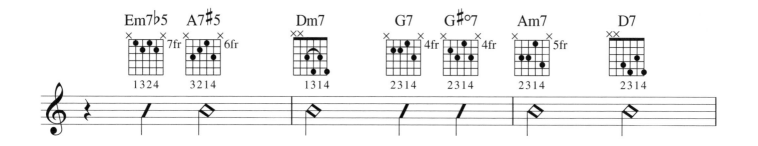

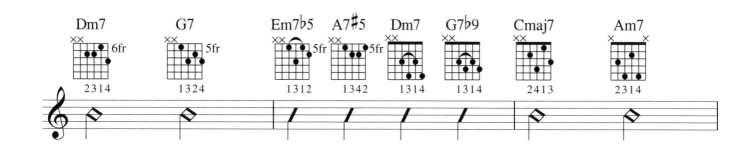

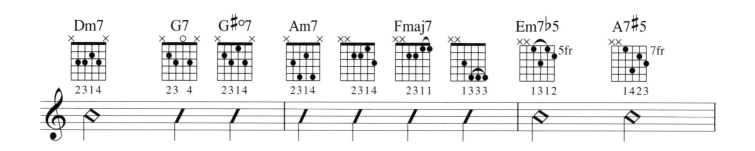

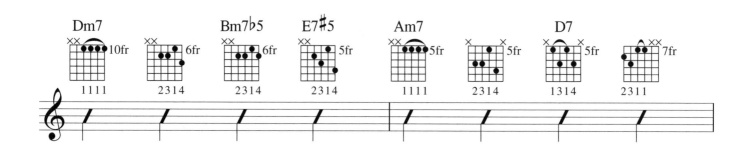

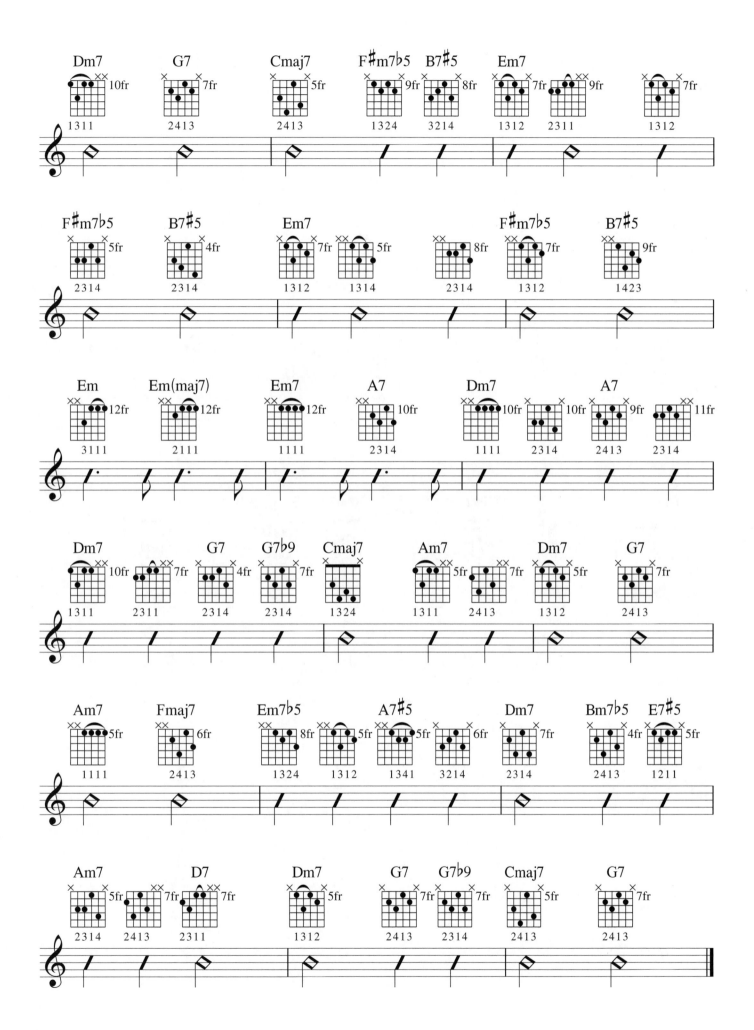

Someday My Prince Will Come

Track 9: Slow Demo
Track 10: Full Speed
Track 11: Full Speed (minus guitar)

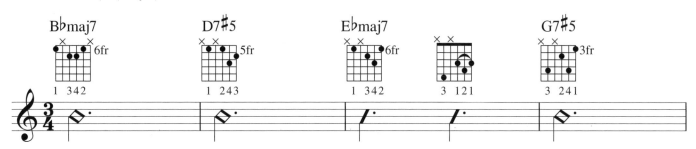

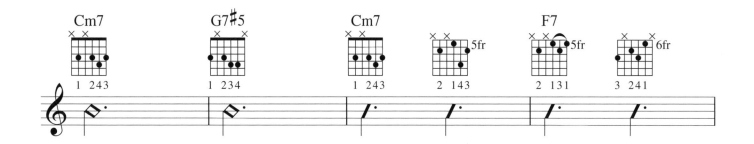

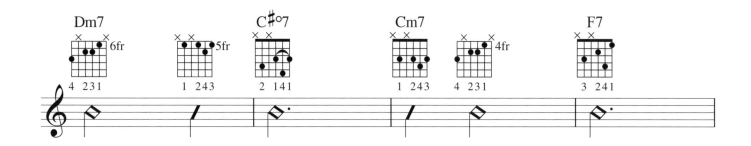

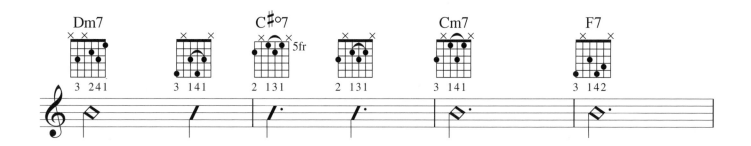

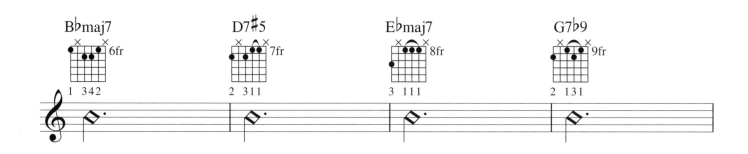

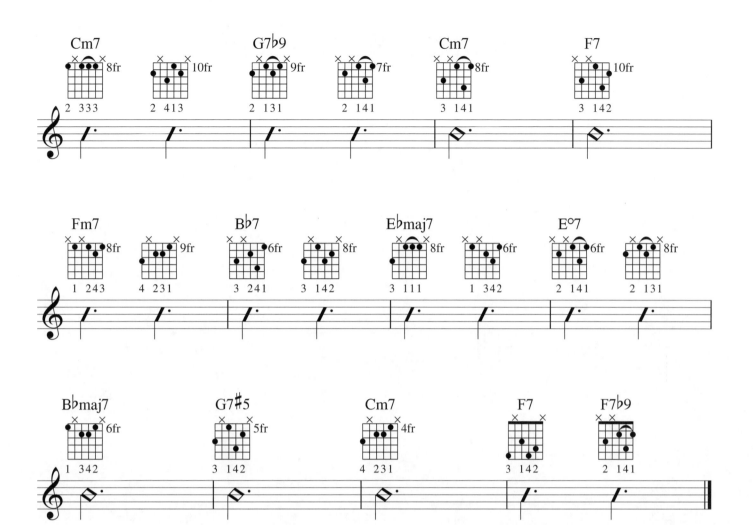

Straight No Chaser

Track 12: Slow Demo
Track 13: Full Speed
Track 14: Full Speed (minus guitar)

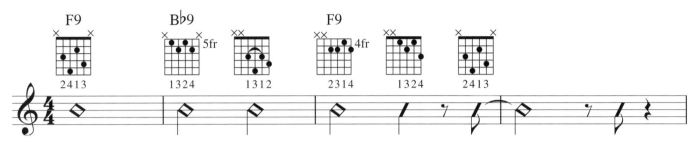

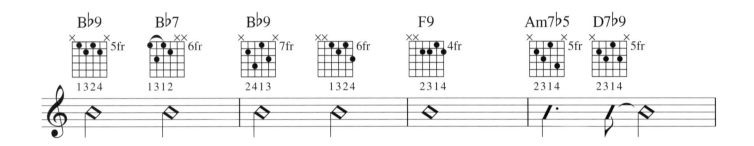

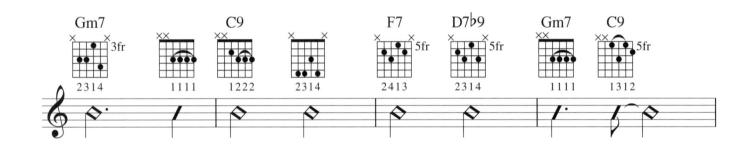

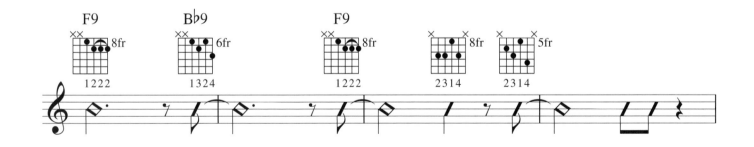

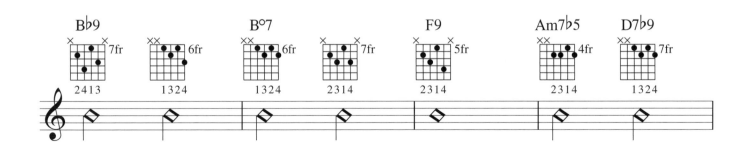

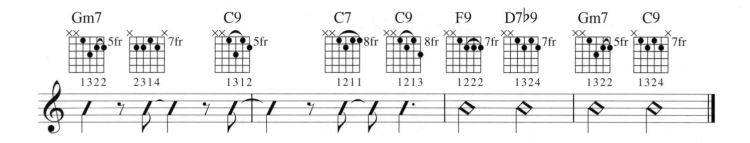

Corcovado

Track 15: Slow Demo
Track 16: Full Speed
Track 17: Full Speed (minus guitar)

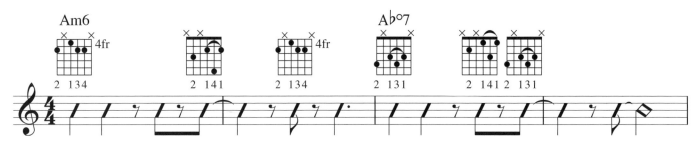

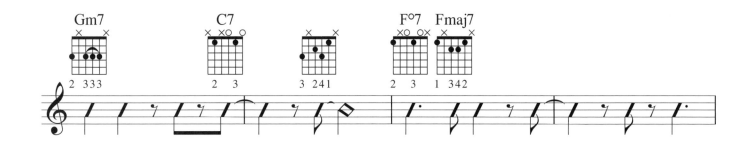

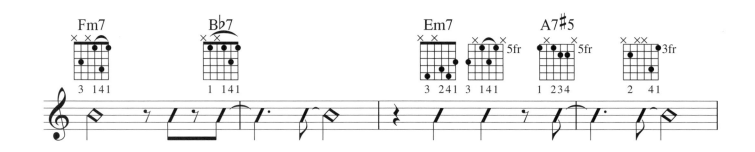

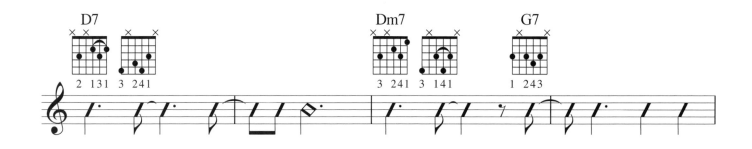

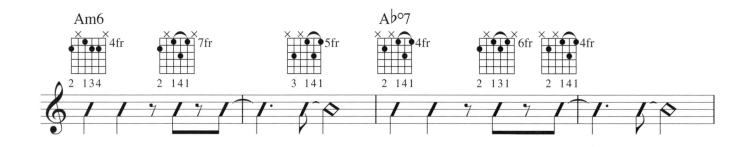

The Days of Wine and Roses

Track 18: Slow Demo
Track 19: Full Speed
Track 20: Full Speed (minus guitar)

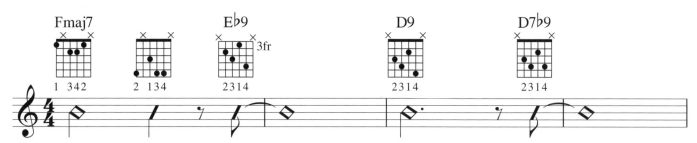

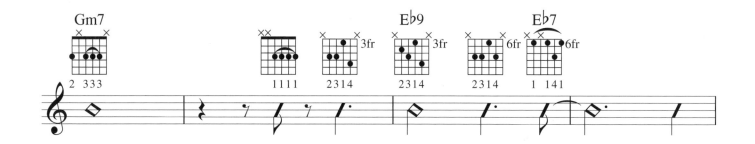

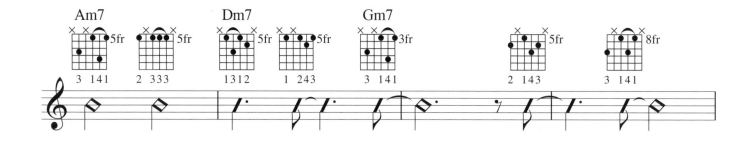

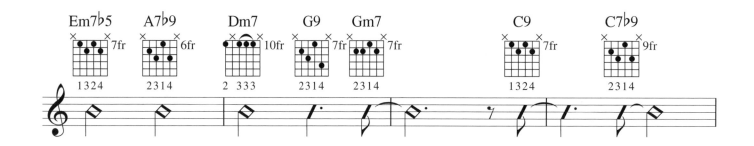

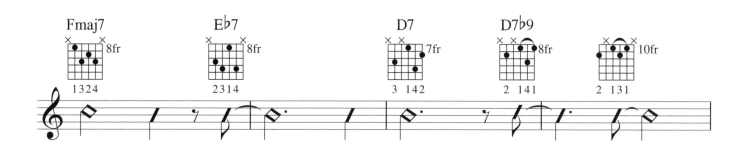

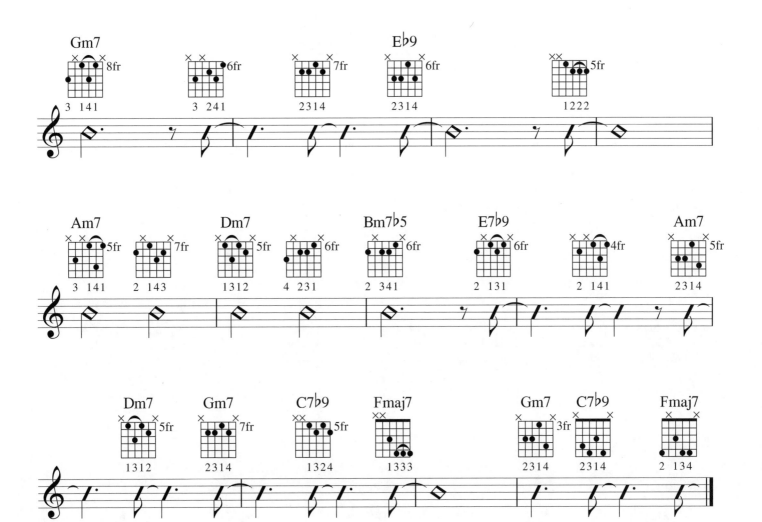

Donna Lee

Track 21: Slow Demo
Track 22: Full Speed
Track 23: Full Speed (minus guitar)

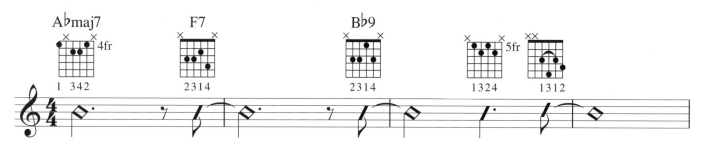

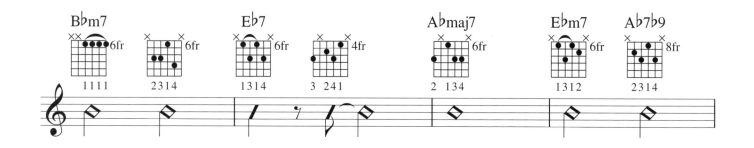

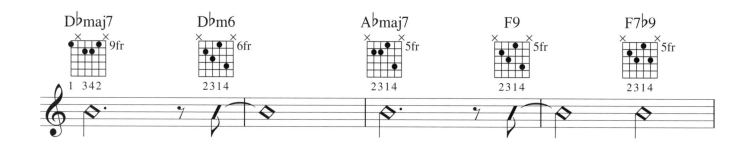

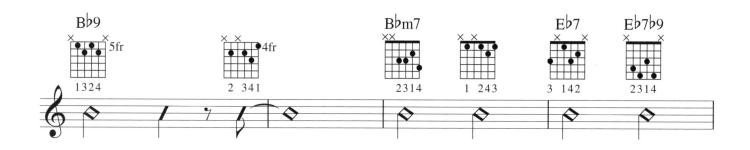

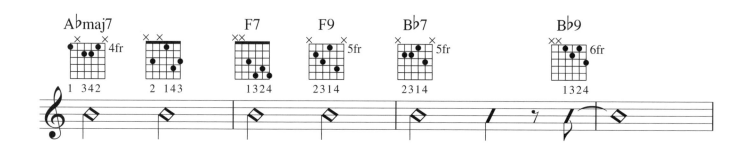

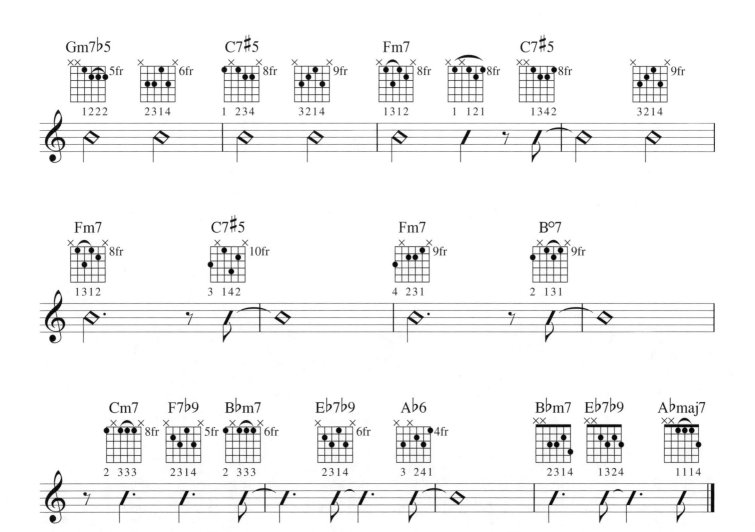

Stella by Starlight

Track 24: Slow Demo
Track 25: Full Speed
Track 26: Full Speed (minus guitar)

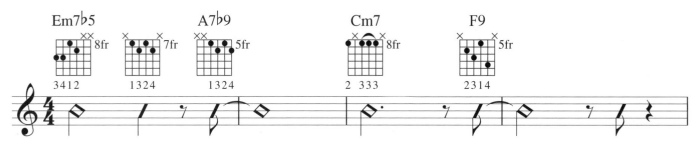

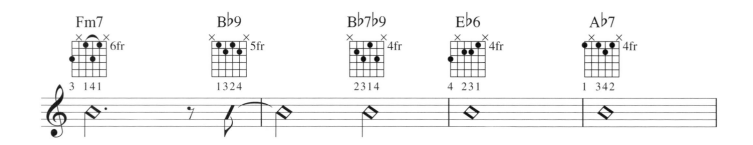

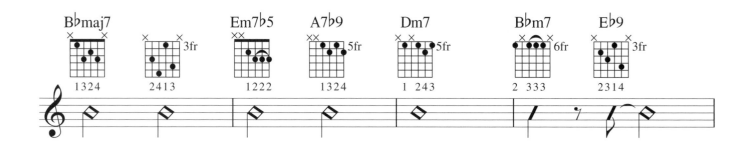

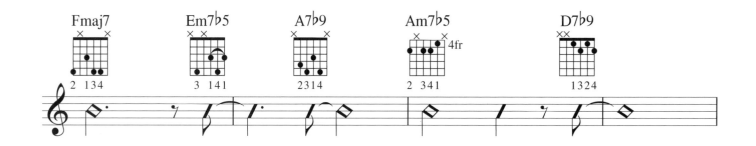

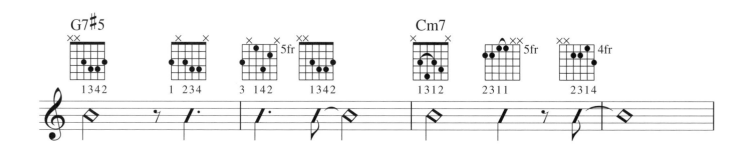

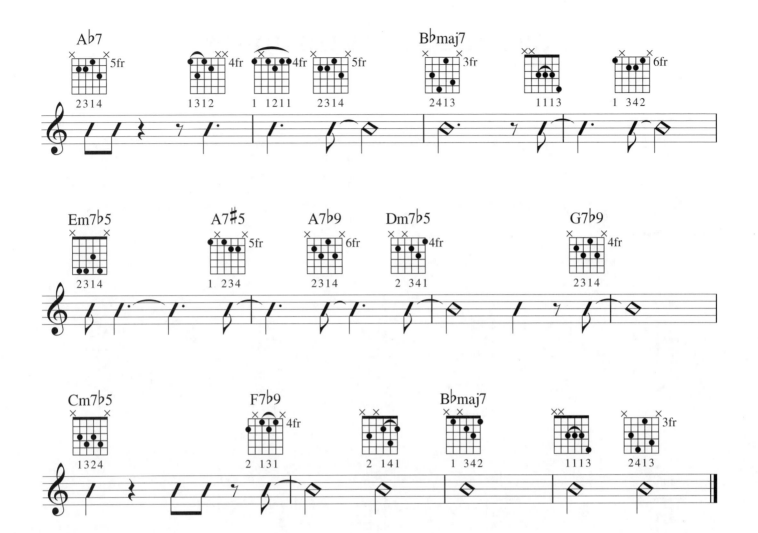

Have You Met Miss Jones?

Track 27: Slow Demo
Track 28: Full Speed
Track 29: Full Speed (minus guitar)

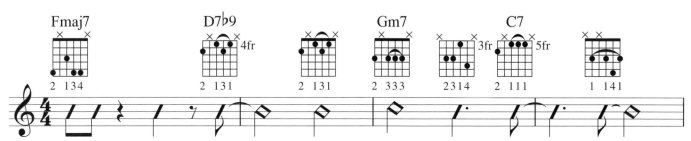

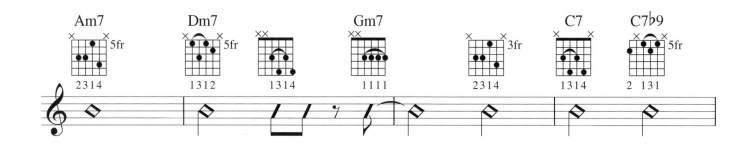

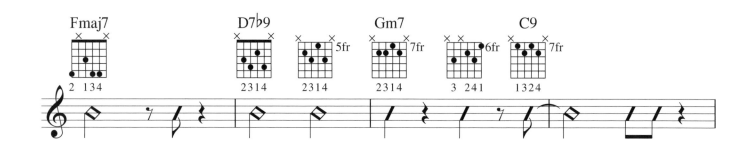

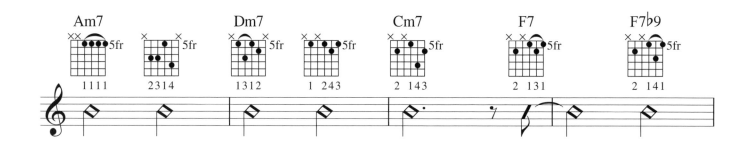

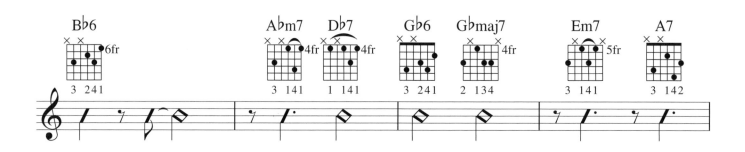

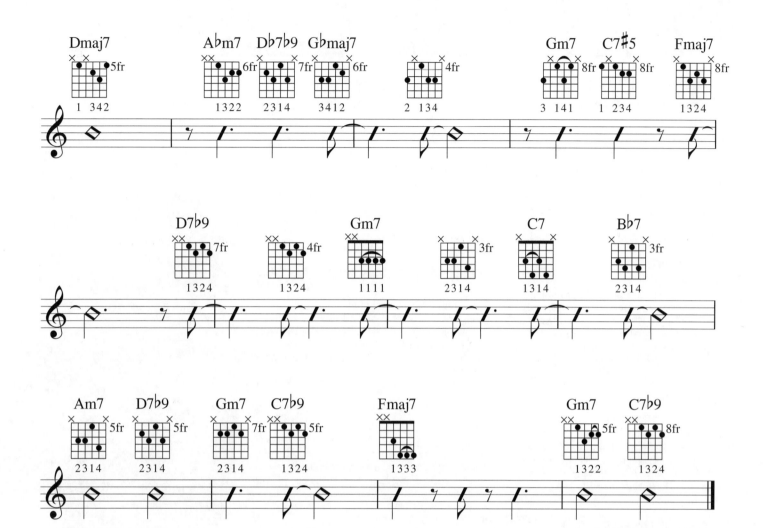

PLAY THE CLASSICS
JAZZ FOLIOS FOR GUITARISTS

BEST OF JAZZ GUITAR
by Wolf Marshall • Signature Licks

In this book/CD pack, Wolf Marshall provides a hands-on analysis of 10 of the most frequently played tunes in the jazz genre, as played by the leading guitarists of all time. Features: All the Things You Are • How Insensitive • I'll Remember April • So What • Yesterdays • and more.
00695586 Book/CD Pack......................................$24.95

GUITAR STANDARDS
Classic Jazz Masters Series

16 classic jazz guitar performances transcribed note for note with tablature: All of You (Kenny Burrell) • Easter Parade (Herb Ellis) • I'll Remember April (Grant Green) • Lover Man (Django Reinhardt) • Song for My Father (George Benson) • The Way You Look Tonight (Wes Montgomery) • and more. Includes a discography.
00699143 Guitar Transcriptions $14.95

JAZZ CLASSICS
Jazz Guitar Chord Melody Solos
arr. Jeff Arnold

27 rich arrangements of jazz classics: Blue in Green • Bluesette • Doxy • Epistrophy • Footprints • Giant Steps • Lush Life • A Night in Tunisia • Nuages • St. Thomas • Waltz for Debby • Yardbird Suite • and more.
00699758 Solo Guitar $14.99

JAZZ CLASSICS FOR SOLO GUITAR
arranged by Robert B. Yelin

This collection includes excellent chord melody arrangements in standard notation and tablature for 35 all-time jazz favorites: April in Paris • Cry Me a River • Day by Day • God Bless' the Child • It Might as Well Be Spring • Lover • My Romance • Nuages • Satin Doll • Tenderly • Unchained Melody • Wave • and more!
00699279 Solo Guitar $17.95

JAZZ FAVORITES FOR SOLO GUITAR
arranged by Robert B. Yelin

This fantastic 35-song collection includes lush chord melody arrangements in standard notation and tab: Autumn in New York • Call Me Irresponsible • How Deep Is the Ocean • I Could Write a Book • The Lady Is a Tramp • Mood Indigo • Polka Dots and Moonbeams • Solitude • Take the "A" Train • Where or When • more.
00699278 Solo Guitar $17.95

JAZZ FOR THE ROCK GUITARIST
by Michael Mueller

Take your playing beyond barre chords and the blues box! This book/CD pack will take you through the essentials of the jazz idiom with plenty of exercises and examples – all of which are demonstrated on the accompanying CD.
00695856 Book/CD Pack......................................$14.95

JAZZ GEMS FOR SOLO GUITAR
arranged by Robert B. Yelin

35 great solo arrangements of jazz classics, including: After You've Gone • Alice in Wonderland • The Christmas Song • Four • Meditation • Stompin' at the Savoy • Sweet and Lovely • Waltz for Debby • Yardbird Suite • You'll Never Walk Alone • You've Changed • and more.
00699617 Solo Guitar $17.95

JAZZ GUITAR BIBLE

The one book that has all of the jazz guitar classics transcribed note-for-note, with standard notation and tablature. Includes over 30 songs: Body and Soul • Girl Talk • I'll Remember April • In a Sentimental Mood • My Funny Valentine • Nuages • Satin Doll • So What • Stardust • Take Five • Tangerine • Yardbird Suite • and more.
00690466 Guitar Recorded Versions $19.95

JAZZ GUITAR CHORD MELODIES
arranged & performed by Dan Towey

This book/CD pack includes complete solo performances of 12 standards, including: All the Things You Are • Body and Soul • My Romance • How Insensitive • My One and Only Love • and more. The arrangements are performance level and range in difficulty from intermediate to advanced.
00698988 Book/CD Pack $19.95

JAZZ GUITAR PLAY-ALONG
Guitar Play-Along Volume 16

With this book/CD pack, all you have to do is follow the tab, listen to the CD to hear how the guitar should sound, and then play along using the separate backing tracks. 8 songs: All Blues • Bluesette • Footprints • How Insensitive (Insensatez) • Misty • Satin Doll • Stella by Starlight • Tenor Madness.
00699584 Book/CD Pack $15.95

JAZZ STANDARDS FOR FINGERSTYLE GUITAR

20 songs, including: All the Things You Are • Autumn Leaves • Bluesette • Body and Soul • Fly Me to the Moon • The Girl from Ipanema • How Insensitive • I've Grown Accustomed to Her Face • My Funny Valentine • Satin Doll • Stompin' at the Savoy • and more.
00699029 Fingerstyle Guitar $10.95

JAZZ STANDARDS FOR SOLO GUITAR
arranged by Robert B. Yelin

35 chord melody guitar arrangements, including: Ain't Misbehavin' • Autumn Leaves • Bewitched • Cherokee • Darn That Dream • Girl Talk • I've Got You Under My Skin • Lullaby of Birdland • My Funny Valentine • A Nightingale Sang in Berkeley Square • Stella by Starlight • The Very Thought of You • and more.
00699277 Solo Guitar $17.95

101 MUST-KNOW JAZZ LICKS
by Wolf Marshall

Add a jazz feel and flavor to your playing! 101 definitive licks, plus a demonstration CD, from every major jazz guitar style, neatly organized into easy-to-use categories. They're all here: swing and pre-bop, bebop, post-bop modern jazz, hard bop and cool jazz, modal jazz, soul jazz and postmodern jazz.
00695433 Book/CD Pack......................................$17.95

FOR MORE INFORMATION, SEE YOUR LOCAL MUSIC DEALER, OR WRITE TO:

HAL•LEONARD®
CORPORATION
7777 W. BLUEMOUND RD. P.O. BOX 13819 MILWAUKEE, WI 53213

Visit Hal Leonard Online at **www.halleonard.com**

Prices, contents and availability subject to change without notice.

1011

JAZZ GUITAR CHORD MELODY SOLOS

This series features chord melody arrangements in standard notation and tablature of songs for intermediate guitarists.

ALL-TIME STANDARDS INCLUDES TAB

27 songs, including: All of Me • Bewitched • Come Fly with Me • A Fine Romance • Georgia on My Mind • How High the Moon • I'll Never Smile Again • I've Got You Under My Skin • It's De-Lovely • It's Only a Paper Moon • My Romance • Satin Doll • The Surrey with the Fringe on Top • Yesterdays • and more.

00699757 Solo Guitar $14.99

CHRISTMAS CAROLS INCLUDES TAB

26 songs, including: Auld Lang Syne • Away in a Manger • Deck the Hall • God Rest Ye Merry, Gentlemen • Good King Wenceslas • Here We Come A-Wassailing • It Came upon the Midnight Clear • Joy to the World • O Holy Night • O Little Town of Bethlehem • Silent Night • Toyland • We Three Kings of Orient Are • and more.

00701697 Solo Guitar $12.99

DISNEY SONGS INCLUDES TAB

27 songs, including: Beauty and the Beast • Can You Feel the Love Tonight • Candle on the Water • Colors of the Wind • A Dream Is a Wish Your Heart Makes • Heigh-Ho • Some Day My Prince Will Come • Under the Sea • When You Wish upon a Star • A Whole New World (Aladdin's Theme) • Zip-A-Dee-Doo-Dah • and more.

00701902 Solo Guitar $14.99

DUKE ELLINGTON INCLUDES TAB

25 songs, including: C-Jam Blues • Caravan • Do Nothin' Till You Hear from Me • Don't Get Around Much Anymore • I Got It Bad and That Ain't Good • I'm Just a Lucky So and So • In a Sentimental Mood • It Don't Mean a Thing (If It Ain't Got That Swing) • Mood Indigo • Perdido • Prelude to a Kiss • Satin Doll • and more.

00700636 Solo Guitar $12.99

FAVORITE STANDARDS INCLUDES TAB

27 songs, including: All the Way • Autumn in New York • Blue Skies • Cheek to Cheek • Don't Get Around Much Anymore • How Deep Is the Ocean • I'll Be Seeing You • Isn't It Romantic? • It Could Happen to You • The Lady Is a Tramp • Moon River • Speak Low • Take the "A" Train • Willow Weep for Me • Witchcraft • and more.

00699756 Solo Guitar $14.99

FINGERPICKING JAZZ STANDARDS INCLUDES TAB

15 songs: Autumn in New York • Body and Soul • Can't Help Lovin' Dat Man • Easy Living • A Fine Romance • Have You Met Miss Jones? • I'm Beginning to See the Light • It Could Happen to You • My Romance • Stella by Starlight • Tangerine • The Very Thought of You • The Way You Look Tonight • When Sunny Gets Blue • Yesterdays.

00699840 Solo Guitar $7.99

JAZZ BALLADS INCLUDES TAB

27 songs, including: Body and Soul • Darn That Dream • Easy to Love (You'd Be So Easy to Love) • Here's That Rainy Day • In a Sentimental Mood • Misty • My Foolish Heart • My Funny Valentine • The Nearness of You • Stella by Starlight • Time After Time • The Way You Look Tonight • When Sunny Gets Blue • and more.

00699755 Solo Guitar $14.99

JAZZ CLASSICS INCLUDES TAB

27 songs, including: Blue in Green • Bluesette • Bouncing with Bud • Cast Your Fate to the Wind • Con Alma • Doxy • Epistrophy • Footprints • Giant Steps • Invitation • Lullaby of Birdland • Lush Life • A Night in Tunisia • Nuages • Ruby, My Dear • St. Thomas • Stolen Moments • Waltz for Debby • Yardbird Suite • and more.

00699758 Solo Guitar $14.99

Prices, content, and availability subject to change without notice. | Disney characters and artwork ©Disney Enterprises, Inc.

HAL•LEONARD®
www.halleonard.com

> "Well-crafted arrangements that sound great and are still accessible to most players."
> – *Guitar Edge* magazine

IMPROVE YOUR IMPROV
AND OTHER JAZZ TECHNIQUES WITH BOOKS FROM HAL LEONARD

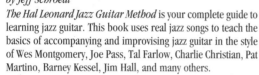

JAZZ GUITAR
Hal Leonard Guitar Method
by Jeff Schroedl

The Hal Leonard Jazz Guitar Method is your complete guide to learning jazz guitar. This book uses real jazz songs to teach the basics of accompanying and improvising jazz guitar in the style of Wes Montgomery, Joe Pass, Tal Farlow, Charlie Christian, Pat Martino, Barney Kessel, Jim Hall, and many others.
00695359 Book/CD Pack... $19.99

AMAZING PHRASING
50 Ways to Improve Your
Improvisational Skills • *by Tom Kolb*

This book/CD pack explores all the main components necessary for crafting well-balanced rhythmic and melodic phrases. It also explains how these phrases are put together to form cohesive solos. Many styles are covered – rock, blues, jazz, fusion, country, Latin, funk and more – and all of the concepts are backed up with musical examples.
00695583 Book/CD Pack... $19.95

BEST OF JAZZ GUITAR
by Wolf Marshall • Signature Licks

In this book/CD pack, Wolf Marshall provides a hands-on analysis of 10 of the most frequently played tunes in the jazz genre, as played by the leading guitarists of all time. Each selection includes technical analysis and performance notes, biographical sketches, and authentic matching audio with backing tracks.
00695586 Book/CD Pack... $24.95

CHORD-MELODY PHRASES FOR GUITAR
by Ron Eschete • REH ProLessons Series

Expand your chord-melody chops with these outstanding jazz phrases! This book covers: chord substitutions, chromatic movements, contrary motion, pedal tones, inner-voice movements, reharmonization techniques, and much more. Includes standard notation and tab, and a CD.
00695628 Book/CD Pack... $17.99

CHORDS FOR JAZZ GUITAR
The Complete Guide to Comping,
Chord Melody and Chord Soloing • *by Charlton Johnson*

This book/CD pack will teach you how to play jazz chords all over the fretboard in a variety of styles and progressions. It covers: voicings, progressions, jazz chord theory, comping, chord melody, chord soloing, voice leading and many more topics. The CD includes 98 full-band demo tracks. No tablature.
00695706 Book/CD Pack... $19.95

CRASH COURSE ON JAZZ GUITAR VOICINGS
The Essential Guide for All Guitarists
by Hugh Burns • Artemis Editions

This ultimate beginner's guide to jazz guitar covers: jazz harmony explained simply, easy essential jazz shapes to get you playing right away, classic jazz progressions, vamps, turnarounds and substitutions and more.
00695815 Book/CD Pack... $9.95

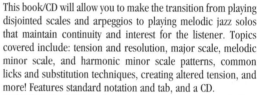

FRETBOARD ROADMAPS – JAZZ GUITAR
The Essential Guitar Patterns
That All the Pros Know and Use • *by Fred Sokolow*

This book/CD pack will get guitarists playing lead & rhythm anywhere on the fretboard, in any key! It teaches a variety of lead guitar styles using moveable patterns, double-note licks, sliding pentatonics and more, through easy-to-follow diagrams and instructions. The CD includes 54 full-demo tracks.
00695354 Book/CD Pack... $14.95

JAZZ IMPROVISATION FOR GUITAR
by Les Wise • REH ProLessons Series

This book/CD will allow you to make the transition from playing disjointed scales and arpeggios to playing melodic jazz solos that maintain continuity and interest for the listener. Topics covered include: tension and resolution, major scale, melodic minor scale, and harmonic minor scale patterns, common licks and substitution techniques, creating altered tension, and more! Features standard notation and tab, and a CD.
00695657 Book/CD Pack... $16.95

JAZZ RHYTHM GUITAR
The Complete Guide
by Jack Grassel

This book/CD pack will help rhythm guitarists better understand: chord symbols and voicings, comping styles and patterns, equipment, accessories and set-up, the fingerboard, chord theory, and much more. The accompanying CD includes 74 full-band tracks.
00695654 Book/CD Pack... $19.95

JAZZ SOLOS FOR GUITAR
Lead Guitar in the Styles of Tal Farlow,
Barney Kessel, Wes Montgomery, Joe Pass, Johnny Smith
by Les Wise

Examine the solo concepts of the masters with this book including phrase-by-phrase performance notes, tips on arpeggio substitution, scale substitution, tension and resolution, jazz-blues, chord soloing, and more. The CD includes full demonstration and rhythm-only tracks.
00695447 Book/CD Pack... $17.95

101 MUST-KNOW JAZZ LICKS
A Quick, Easy Reference Guide
for All Guitarists • *by Wolf Marshall*

Here are 101 definitive licks, plus a demonstration CD, from every major jazz guitar style, neatly organized into easy-to-use categories. They're all here: swing and pre-bop, bebop, post-bop modern jazz, hard bop and cool jazz, modal jazz, soul jazz and postmodern jazz. Includes an introduction, tips for using the book/CD, and a list of suggested recordings.
00695433 Book/CD Pack... $17.95

SWING AND BIG BAND GUITAR
Four-to-the-Bar Comping in the Style of
Freddie Green • *by Charlton Johnson*

This unique package teaches the essentials of swing and big band styles, including chord voicings, inversions, substitutions; time and groove, reading charts, chord reduction, and expansion; sample songs, patterns, progressions, and exercises; chord reference library; and a CD with over 50 full-demo examples. Uses chord grids – no tablature.
00695147 Book/CD Pack... $19.99

For More Information, See Your Local Music Dealer,
Or Write To:

HAL•LEONARD® CORPORATION
7777 W. Bluemound Rd. P.O. Box 13819 Milwaukee, WI 53213

Visit Hal Leonard Online at **www.halleonard.com**

*Prices, contents and availability
subject to change without notice.*